impact

4

G000272599

SERIES EDITORS
JoAnn (Jodi) Crandall
Joan Kang Shin

AUTHOR
Thomas Fast

NATIONAL GEOGRAPHIC LEARNING | CENGAGE Learning®

Australia • Brazil • Mexico • Singapore • United Kingdom • United States

Thank you to the educators who provided invaluable feedback during the development of *Impact*:

EXPERT PANEL

Márcia Ferreira, Academic Coordinator, CCBEU, Franca, Brazil

Jianwei Song, Vice-general Manager, Ensure International Education, Harbin, China

María Eugenia Flores, Academic Director, and **Liana Rojas-Binda**, Head of Recruitment & Training, Centro Cultural Costarricense-Norteamericano, San José, Costa Rica

Liani Setiawati, M.Pd., SMPK 1 BPK PENABUR Bandung, Bandung, Indonesia

Micaela Fernandes, Head of Research and Development Committee and Assessment Committee, Pui Ching Middle School, Macau

Héctor Sánchez Lozano, Academic Director, and **Carolina Tripodi**, Head of the Juniors Program, Proulex, Guadalajara, Mexico

Rosario Giraldez, Academic Director, Alianza Cultural, Montevideo, Uruguay

REVIEWERS

BRAZIL

Renata Cardoso, Colégio do Sol, Guara, DF

Fábio Delano Vidal Carneiro, Colégio Sete de Setembro, Fortaleza

Cristiano Carvalho, Centro Educacional Leonardo da Vinci, Vitória

Silvia Corrêa, Associação Alumni, São Paulo

Carol Espinosa, Associação Cultural Brasil Estados Unidos, Salvador

Marcia Ferreira, Centro Cultural Brasil Estados Unidos, Franca

Clara Haddad, ELT Consultant, São Paulo

Elaine Carvalho Chaves Hodgson, Colégio Militar de Brasília, Brasília

Thays Farias Galvão Ladosky, Associação Brasil América, Recife

Itana Lins, Colégio Anchieta, Salvador

Samantha Mascarenhas, Associação Cultural Brasil Estados Unidos, Salvador

Ann Marie Moreira, Pan American School of Bahia, Bahia

Rodrigo Ramirez, CEETEPS- Fatec Zona Sul, São Paulo

Paulo Torres, Vitória Municipality, Vitória

Renata Zainotte, Go Up Idiomas, Rio de Janeiro

CHINA

Zhou Chao, MaxEn Education, Beijing

Zhu Haojun, Only International Education, Shanghai

Su Jing, Beijing Chengxun International English School, Beijing

Jianjun Shen, Phoenix City International School, Guangzhou

COSTA RICA

Luis Antonio Quesada-Umaña, Centro Cultural Costarricense Norteamericano, San José

INDONESIA

Luz S. Ismail, M.A., LIA Institute of Language and Vocational Training, Jakarta

Selestin Zainuddin, LIA Institute of Language and Vocational Training, Jakarta

Rosalia Dian Devitasari, SMP Kolese Kanisius, Jakarta

JAPAN

John Williams, Tezukayama Gakuen, Nara

MEXICO

Nefertiti González, Instituto Mexicano Madero, Puebla

Eugenia Islas, Instituto Tlalpan, Mexico City

Marta MM Seguí, Colegio Velmont A.C., Puebla

SOUTH KOREA

Min Yuol (Alvin) Cho, Global Leader English Education, Yong In

THAILAND

Panitnan Kalayanapong, Eduzone Co., Ltd., Bangkok

TURKEY

Damla Çaltuğ, İELEV, Istanbul

Basak Nalcakar Demiralp, Ankara Sinav College, Ankara

Humeyra Olcayli, İstanbul Bilim College, Istanbul

VIETNAM

Chantal Kruger, ILA Vietnam, Hô Chí Minh

Ai Nguyen Huynh, Vietnam USA Society, Hô Chí Minh

impact

4

Unit 1

CORY RICHARDS **Photojournalist**

Cory Richards takes pictures all over the world. He uses these photos to tell stories about people and places around the world. He's been to all seven continents, climbed some of the tallest mountains on Earth and hiked in below-freezing temperatures. Cory has overcome extreme obstacles and has pushed himself to his limit. He doesn't mind being out of his comfort zone. Do you?

Unit 2

PATRICK MEIER **Crisis Mapper**

Did you know that social media posts, text messages and emails can save lives? Thanks to crisis mappers like Patrick Meier, people affected by natural disasters can get help faster. Patrick sorts through their communication and creates crisis maps that he shares with rescue teams. Patrick believes that, when people collaborate and use technology, they can make a difference.

Unit 3

BARTON SEAVER **Chef/Conservationist**

Barton Seaver wants you to think about what you eat. As a chef and conservationist, Barton has travelled all over the world to cook and eat different foods. He likes to learn about people and cultures through food. Now he works to raise awareness about healthy eating and seafood sustainability.

Unit 4

JACK JOHNSON **Musician**

Jack Johnson is a musician, surfer and environmentalist. He uses his music to promote sustainability and conservation. Jack travels to his concerts in biofuel buses and promotes sustainable local food at his shows. Jack proves that being green and having fun can go hand-in-hand. What do you like to do for 'green fun'?

Unit 5

COREY JASKOLSKI Engineer/Inventor

Corey Jaskolski is an engineer who creates technologies so that people can virtually explore the world. With his 360-degree camera, anyone can explore inside of King Tut's tomb without harming its artefacts or swim in the deep sea alongside the sharks without leaving home. Corey's gadgets help explorers protect what they discover. Do you use technology to explore?

Unit 6

NIZAR IBRAHIM Palaeontologist

Nizar Ibrahim is German/Moroccan and as a child in Germany, he wanted to learn about dinosaurs. He's lucky because now that's his job as he searches for dinosaurs in Morocco. He decided to hunt for dinosaurs there because very little research has been done in the Sahara Desert. Imagine how excited he was to find fossils of a prehistoric giant, *Spinosaurus*.

Unit 7

TAN LE Innovator/Entrepreneur

Have you ever wanted to be able to move objects with your mind? Tan Le created a portable brain scanner that can do just that! It also helps doctors better understand the healthy human brain. Tan went through a long process of trial and error before her brain scanner worked, which taught her that failure is a step toward success.

Unit 8

STEPHEN ALVAREZ Photographer

Photographer Stephen Alvarez believes art has the power to connect people across time and distance – even from the prehistoric world to people today. In 2014, he photographed ancient art in the Chauvet-Pont-d'Arc cave in France. These paintings were made 36,000 years ago! Stephen felt very connected to the ancient artists that created them. Does art help you connect with others?

Pushing the Limits

Free-climbing the Dawn Wall in
Yosemite National Park, United States

'We have to learn how far we can go.'
Cory Richards

TO START

1. Look at the climber. Why would he choose to climb this rock? What are some of the risks he faces?

2. What is the most challenging sport you've ever tried?

3. Why should we challenge ourselves? What is a benefit of taking risks?

Have you ever **pushed yourself** to your **limit**? Do you know anyone who has? Do you ever wonder what can be gained by climbing a tall cliff – or jumping off it? Why do something that causes the body **pain**?

People can be transformed by pushing themselves. These experiences teach **determination**. Often, the desire to achieve our goal **enables** us to take risks. Many people take mild risks. Others feel a need to reach the unreachable. These **extreme** athletes test their own **mental** and **physical** boundaries.

In most traditional sports, athletes compete against one another. But in extreme sports, the biggest **opponent** is nature. In this photo, Olympic snowboarder Jussi Oksanen glides down the side of a glacier. Snowboarding on solid ice is **hazardous**, especially with a 12 m. (40 ft.) drop below the glacier! But for extreme athletes like Oksanen, risk is just part of the job.

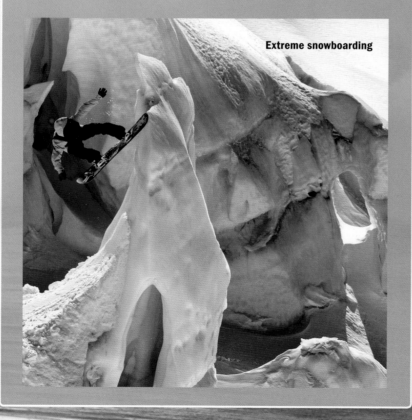

Extreme snowboarding

The same is true for big-wave surfers. Animals such as sharks and jellyfish pose serious risks to surfers. Another **obstacle** that surfers must **overcome** is the force of the water. After this photo was taken, surfer Koa Rothman was taken under by the unbelievable force of the wave. So why do it? 'The view I had right here was one of the most amazing things I have ever seen in my life,' says Koa. 'Being in the middle of all that energy is unexplainable!'

Athletes who participate in the *Marathon des Sables*, or MdS, need to have incredible **endurance**. In this desert marathon, participants must cross a distance of approximately 250 km. (155 mi.) over five or six days. The event takes place in the Sahara Desert, where temperatures can reach more than 50°C (122°F). It's no wonder that the MdS is considered the toughest race on Earth!

The athletes shown in the photos are **role models** for anyone seeking adventure. Do they inspire you to push your own limits?

Desert-marathon running

Big-wave surfing

2 **LEARN NEW WORDS** Listen and repeat. 🎧003

3 **Work in pairs.** Which of these sports would you try? Why would you try it? What risks would you face?

4 **Read and write the words from the list.** Make any necessary changes.

determination	hazardous	mental	obstacle	opponent
overcome	pain	physical	push himself	role model

Photographer and adventurer Cory Richards is used to difficult conditions. Cory has _____ many difficult _____ to bring us some incredible outdoor action photography. Cory believes that pushing his _____ and _____ limits helps him to better connect with himself and with the world.

In 2011, Cory successfully climbed an 8,000 m. (26,000 ft.) peak in the middle of winter. However, due to the _____ conditions, this challenge nearly cost him his life. On the way down, Cory and his team were caught in a major avalanche. 'Once the avalanche took us, there was no more fear,' says Cory. Although this experience scared him, he still takes risks to get a great photo. Cory's _____ and endurance make him a great _____ .

5 **LEARN NEW WORDS** Listen to the words and match them to the definitions. Then listen and repeat. 🎧 004 005

achieve	boundary	unbelievable	unreachable

_____ 1. incredible

_____ 2. limit

_____ 3. gain through hard work or effort

_____ 4. impossible

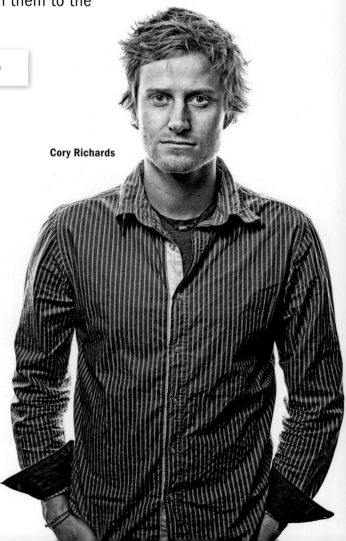

Cory Richards

6 **YOU DECIDE** Choose an activity. Work in pairs.

1. Talk about characteristics that adventurers like Cory need to have. Which of these characteristics do you have? Which would you like to have?

2. Role-play an interview between a TV reporter and an extreme athlete who has just completed a new challenge.

3. Invent an extreme sport. Work together to make a poster describing a competition for this sport.

Showing interest in a conversation

Statement	Responses
I love surfing.	Wow! What's that like?
	Really! I never knew that <u>you could surf</u>.
	What can you tell me about <u>surfing</u>?
	Tell me more about <u>how you learnt to surf</u>.
	What about you? Do you like <u>extreme sports</u>?
	You're <u>a surfer</u>? Me, too!

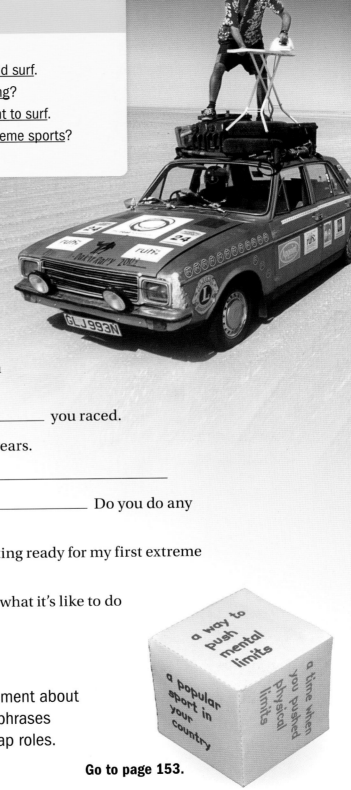

1 **Listen.** How do these speakers show interest in the conversation? Write the phrases you hear. ∩007

2 **Read and complete the dialogue.**

Lee: What are you doing, Jon?

Jon: I'm getting ready for my next mountain bike race.

Lee: Really! _____ you raced.

Jon: Yeah, I've been racing for about three years.

Lee: _____

Jon: It's very cool. _____ Do you do any extreme sports?

Lee: Yeah, I like rock climbing. And I'm getting ready for my first extreme ironing competition.

Jon: _____ what it's like to do extreme ironing.

Lee: I can't yet – I've never done it!

3 **Work in pairs.** Throw the cube. Make a statement about the topic on the cube. Your partner uses the phrases above to maintain the conversation. Then swap roles.

a way to push mental limits

a popular sport in your country

a time when you pushed physical limits

Go to page 153.

4 **Work in groups.** Do you take risks? Share stories about risks you have taken. Tell one true story and one false story. See if your group can guess the true story. Use the phrases above to maintain the conversations.

GRAMMAR 🎧008

Embedded clauses, questions and commands

I think ... Extreme sports are dangerous.	**I think extreme sports are** dangerous.
I wonder ... What obstacles has Cory overcome?	**I wonder what obstacles Cory has overcome.**
Do you know ... Can we climb that mountain in winter?	**Do you know if we can climb** that mountain in winter?
I'm asking you ... Try downhill mountain biking.	**I'm asking you to try** downhill mountain biking.

1 **Work independently.** Listen to the speakers. Then complete the embedded clause, question or command. Remember to change the order of words when necessary. 🎧009

1. She's guessing _____

2. He's wondering _____

3. You're telling me _____

4. I think _____

5. I'm asking you _____

2 **Work in pairs.** Make sentences to form embedded clauses, questions and commands.

I wonder	Wear a helmet when you ride your bike.
I think	Had Cory been in an avalanche before?
I'm asking	Teach your brother how to surf.
I'm telling	How many countries has Cory visited?
Do you remember if	You could try ice climbing.

1. _____

2. _____

3. _____

4. _____

5. _____

3 **LEARN NEW WORDS You've learnt about physical challenges.** Now listen and read about a mental challenge. Then listen and repeat. 🎧 010 011

A **non-traditional** sport, such as ice climbing, can really push us to our physical limits. But have you ever done anything that pushes you to your mental limits? Around the world, students participate in tough academic competitions, such as Maths Olympiads. These **events** require a lot of training, just as an extreme sport does. The competitions often require students to **struggle** with complex problems. Sometimes it takes over an hour to complete just one!

Nur Muhammad Shafiullah knows first-hand how the Maths Olympiads can push mental limits. He is the youngest student ever to compete in the International Mathematical Olympiad. At 15, Nur Muhammad went to the international competition to **represent** his native country, Bangladesh. He competed against students from 125 countries and took the bronze medal! The next year he did it again. The year after that he earnt a silver medal. Nur Muhammad's maths skills are really unbelievable. What about you? Do you think the International Mathematical Olympiad is beyond your mental limits?

4 **Work in pairs.** Write sentences using the words below. Include an embedded clause, question or command in each sentence.

1. wonder / time / event 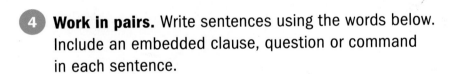 I wonder if the event takes much time.

2. guessing / struggle / difficult _____

3. think / student / prepare _____

4. telling / non-traditional / sport _____

5. asking / represent / country _____

5 **Work in groups.** Think of other competitions that provide mental challenges. What do you know about them? What questions do you have? Discuss in your group, using embedded clauses, questions and commands as much as possible.

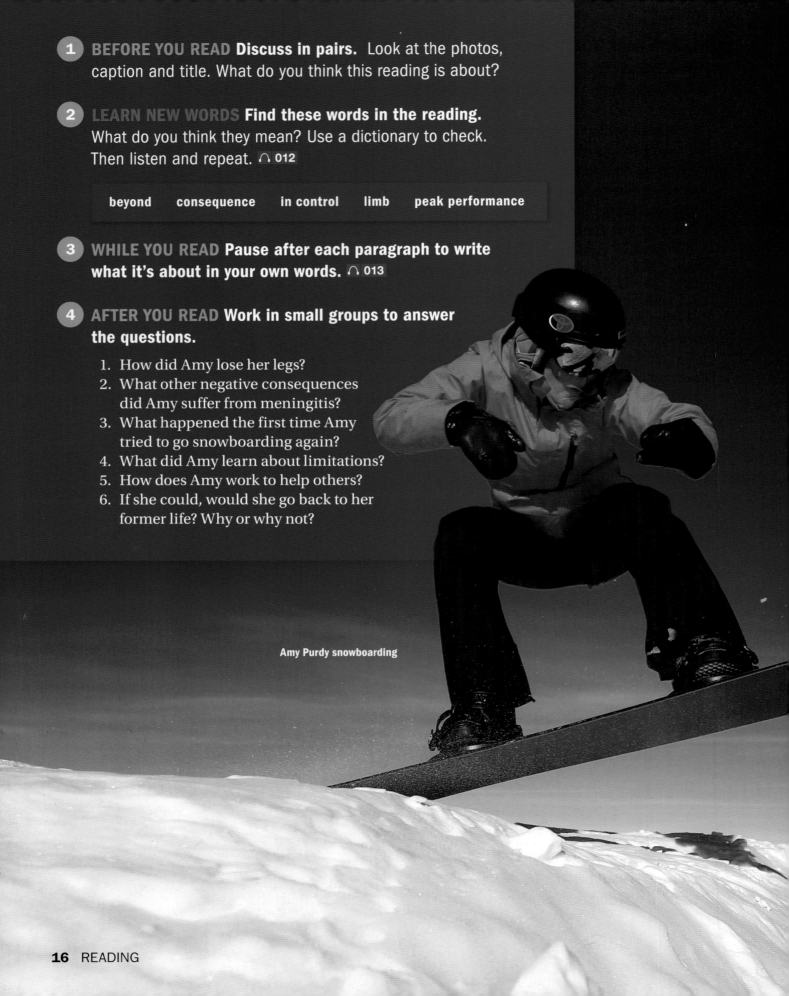

1 BEFORE YOU READ **Discuss in pairs.** Look at the photos, caption and title. What do you think this reading is about?

2 LEARN NEW WORDS **Find these words in the reading.** What do you think they mean? Use a dictionary to check. Then listen and repeat. ∩ 012

| beyond | consequence | in control | limb | peak performance |

3 WHILE YOU READ **Pause after each paragraph to write what it's about in your own words.** ∩ 013

4 AFTER YOU READ **Work in small groups to answer the questions.**

1. How did Amy lose her legs?
2. What other negative consequences did Amy suffer from meningitis?
3. What happened the first time Amy tried to go snowboarding again?
4. What did Amy learn about limitations?
5. How does Amy work to help others?
6. If she could, would she go back to her former life? Why or why not?

Amy Purdy snowboarding

No Limits

AMY PURDY SEES HER LIMITATIONS AS A GIFT THAT HAS HELPED HER DO AMAZING THINGS.

Amy Purdy is a world-class athlete, model and actress. She has achieved amazing success in her life and hasn't let anything slow her down – even the loss of both legs! In fact, some of Amy's greatest achievements came after she lost them.

When Amy was 15, she started snowboarding. After finishing high school, she moved to the mountains, where she could easily spend her free time snowboarding. She felt totally in control of her life. But then at 19, she contracted meningitis, a horrible disease that left her with only a two per cent chance of survival. Amy survived, but there were terrible consequences. She lost a kidney, the hearing in her left ear, and both legs below the knees.

For a long time Amy felt depressed. But when she closed her eyes, she could still see herself snowboarding. She decided not to let this situation take over her life. By the time she was 21, she was back on her board, wearing artificial legs she had built herself. The first time she tried to use them, she fell off, but her legs kept going down the hill without her! After a few years of hard training using her new legs, Amy was able to reach her peak performance level. She became the Para-Snowboarding World Champion in 2012, and she later won the bronze medal in the 2014 Paralympic Games.

Amy's new life was beyond what she expected. Suddenly, she had become a celebrity, a fashion model and an actress. She was even on the popular American TV programme *Dancing with the Stars*. Most importantly, she started helping people like her to do the sports they love. She started a company that makes artificial limbs, and she created an organisation that introduces people with physical disabilities to action sports.

Now, if you ask Amy, 'Would you want to change your situation?', she would say no. Losing her legs has enabled, not disabled, her. According to Amy, 'It's facing our fears head on that allows us to live our lives beyond our borders.'

5 **Work in pairs.** Re-read the text. Then without looking, take turns saying what you remember. Use your own words.

6 **Discuss in groups.**

1. How did getting meningitis impact Amy's life? Identify positive and negative impacts.
2. Do you agree that disadvantages can become advantages? Explain.
3. Do you think anyone can overcome an obstacle like Amy has? Why or why not? Give examples.

1 **BEFORE YOU WATCH** **Discuss in pairs.**

1. Describe a time when you experienced an uncomfortable or dangerous situation.

2. What do you do when you feel stressed? What do you think Cory does?

3. Think of a photo that has taught you something. Describe the photo and what you learnt from it.

2 **Work in pairs.** The title of this video is *A Tribute to Discomfort*. Using the title and what you already know about Cory, predict what you think the video will be about.

3 **WHILE YOU WATCH** **Take notes.** Preview the questions in Activity 4. Watch scene 1.1.

4 **AFTER YOU WATCH** **Discuss in pairs.**

1. What is adventure for Cory?

2. Why does Cory take photos in extreme places?

3. What is Cory's most important tool for connecting with the people he photographs?

4. How has Cory's photography changed since he started?

5 **Work in pairs.** Cory says that education can come from observing. With a partner, take time to really observe another person, animal or group. Look closely at all of the details. Then write a list of five things that you noticed by closely observing. Discuss what you wrote. Take note of what surprises you.

6 **Work in groups.** In the video, Cory mentions the 'richness of struggle'. Try something that will cause you to struggle or to be uncomfortable. Discuss the positives of this experience.

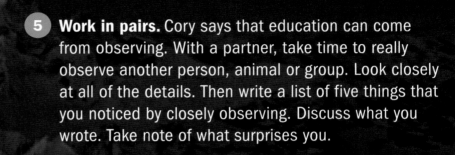

Cory Richards takes risks to get a good shot. This photo was taken from the top of the 8,034 m. (26,360 ft.) Gasherbrum II, in Pakistan.

7 **YOU DECIDE** **Choose an activity. Work in pairs.**

1. Research Cory's photography. Share and describe your favourites of his photos with the class.

2. Photography gives Cory a voice. Take a photograph to teach others about someone or something. Share your photo with a partner. Discuss your partner's reactions.

3. Compare and contrast Amy Purdy and Cory Richards. How does each person push him/herself? What obstacles has each person overcome?

Adding emphasis

My sister loves hiking in the Himalayas.
The place (where) my sister loves hiking
is the Himalayas.

I won't go surfing. I don't like swimming
in the sea.
The reason (why) I won't go surfing **is that** I
don't like swimming in the sea.

He loves yoga because it makes him feel relaxed.
The thing (that) he loves about yoga **is that** it
makes him feel relaxed.

I like snow kiting. It pushes me to my
physical limits.
What I like best about snow kiting **is that** it
pushes me to my physical limits.

1 **Read.** Then rewrite the sentences to add emphasis.

1. I prefer snowboarding to skiing because I need less equipment.

   The reason why _I prefer snowboarding is that I need less equipment._

2. José really enjoys climbing in the Andes.

   The place _____

3. I love the excitement of kite surfing.

   The thing _____

4. Maria likes trying extreme sports.

   The person _____

5. You should try *tae kwon do*. It really helps you focus.

   The reason _____

2 **Work in pairs.** Take turns choosing cards from each pile. Discuss the sport pictured on your card. Add emphasis.

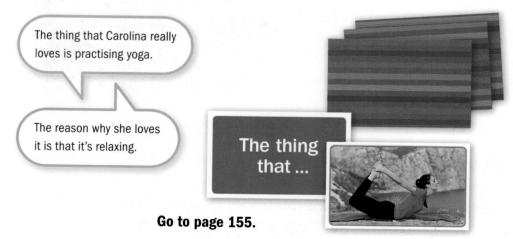

The thing that Carolina really loves is practising yoga.

The reason why she loves it is that it's relaxing.

The thing that ...

Go to page 155.

WRITING

A biography tells the story of a person's life. Here are some useful words and phrases to connect ideas when writing a biography:

afterwards	**at first**	**eventually**
later on	**more recently**	**ultimately**

1 **Read the model.** Work in pairs to study the writing model. What words does the writer use to organise the biography? Underline them.

Yuko Arimori is an Olympic marathon runner. She was born in Japan in 1966. At first, Arimori had difficulty walking because of a problem with her legs. Other children made fun of her. Her gym teacher helped her to gain confidence, and Arimori learnt to try new things such as track running. Through hard work, she became one of the best high school runners in her city.

Eventually, Arimori tried to join a top track team in Japan. When a spot opened for a marathon runner, Arimori saw her chance. She had never been fast, but speed wasn't as important as endurance, which Arimori had. Ultimately, she became one of the best female marathon runners in the world. In 1992, at the age of 26, she participated in the Barcelona Olympics, where she won the silver medal. Afterwards, in the 1996 Olympics, Arimori won the bronze.

Later on, in 1998, Arimori decided to go beyond just running. She started Hearts of Gold, a volunteer organisation to help land mine victims in Cambodia. Hearts of Gold sponsors the Angkor Wat International Half Marathon. Runners from around the world compete to raise money to buy artificial limbs for those who lost arms and legs because of land mines. In fact, many of the victims join the race!

More recently, Arimori was a United Nations Goodwill Ambassador. Today, she's the President and CEO of Special Olympics Nippon. She continues to help people in Cambodia and other parts of the world.

2 **Work in pairs.** Identify four phases of Yuko's life.

3 **Write.** Write a biography of an athlete who is a role model for others. Use the words and phrases above to help you organise the biography.

Test Your Limits

'Adventure is anything that puts us outside our comfort zone.'

Cory Richards
National Geographic Photography Fellow, Photojournalist

1. Watch scene 1.2.

2. Cory gets out of his comfort zone by climbing the tallest mountains in the world – in the winter! What takes you out of your comfort zone? Discuss with a partner.

3. How could you get more adventure from your life? What do you think you might learn about yourself by trying something new?

Make an Impact

YOU DECIDE Choose a project.

1 Try something new!

· Do something you've never done before.

· Write a paragraph to describe your experiences. What did you do? Did it take you outside of your comfort zone? What were the benefits and challenges of this new experience?

· Present a summary of your experience to the class.

2 Create an instructional video.

· Choose a particular sport that pushes your limits, such as yoga, martial arts or distance running.

· Create a video about the sport. Describe how to do the sport. Talk about its mental and physical requirements.

· Film your video and share it with the class.

3 Interview a role model.

· Choose a person in your community who is a role model for teens.

· Write at least five questions to use in your interview. Ask about the person's life, what obstacles he/she has overcome, and how he/she has pushed him/herself.

· Conduct your interview. Then summarise what you learnt about the person for your classmates. Share a photo if possible.

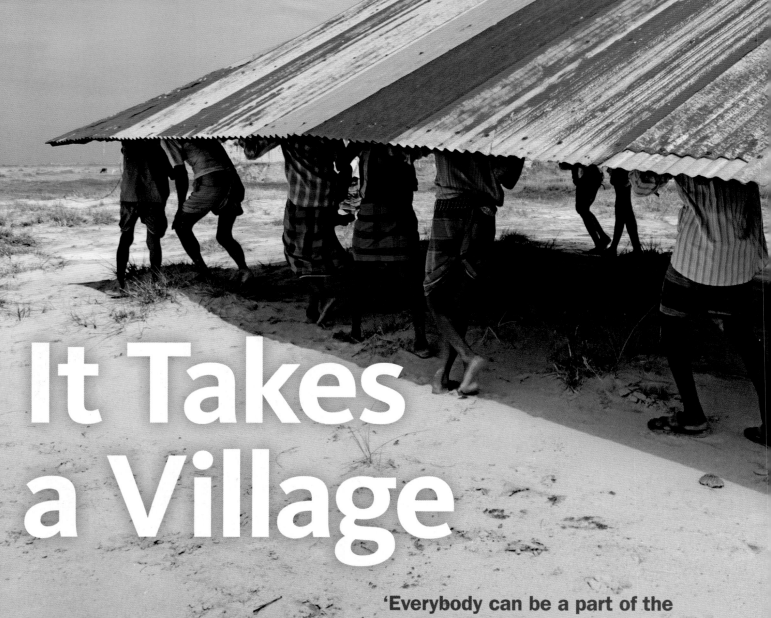

It Takes a Village

'Everybody can be a part of the solution if they want.'

Patrick Meier

Men working together to move a roof, Bangladesh

TO START

1. What are the people in the photo doing? Why might they be doing this?

2. Think of a time when you needed someone else's help. Describe the problem. Who helped you? How did they help?

3. People need help after a crisis, such as an earthquake or a powerful storm. What types of things do people need in these situations? How could you help them?

1 **How can we help people we don't know? Why would we want to?**
Discuss. Then listen and read. 🎧 015

We want to help each other in times of **crisis**. This idea is nothing new. For centuries, our ancestors have worked together to help one another whenever a crisis struck their village. This collaboration brought their communities together. Over time, these communities have **expanded** to become a 'global village' of over seven billion people. When we hear about a massive earthquake or typhoon hitting another part of the world, we still want to help – but how? Crisis mapper Patrick Meier has found a way you can help – without even leaving your home.

Meier has created a network of 'digital **humanitarians**', who produce crisis maps that **measure** the **scale** of a disaster and provide the most up-to-date information for what is needed on the ground. They do it through **crowdsourcing**, or transmitting information using online resources and social media.

Storm Warning Data Execute S
45127875454561121456421 Lo

Patrick Meier analyses data to help with relief efforts during a storm.

People in the affected area **upload** messages and photos that show **evidence** of disasters immediately after they occur. These updates **generate** an enormous **amount** of **data**, which is sorted by digital humanitarians and then posted to the crisis map. People working online and on the ground **process** the information and use it to understand **the big picture**. Rescuers use these updates to **monitor** the levels of destruction and co-ordinate relief for difficult situations. So now when disaster strikes, help can come from anywhere on Earth.

2 **LEARN NEW WORDS Listen and repeat.**
🎧 016

3 **Work in pairs.** Have you ever helped anyone in need? What did you do? Would you use social media to help people you've never met? Why or why not?

4 **Read and listen.** Write the missing words and phrases. ∩ 017

Patrick Meier uses _____ maps and social media to organise information and give _____ on what's happening at a disaster site. However, scientists are using other forms of technology to collect _____ , to _____ solutions and to help people in need. Some scientists are developing microbots to explore where humans cannot easily go, such as outer space or inside the human body. Microbots are simple machines, but when released in large _____ , they can accomplish a lot. If sent into a disaster area, scientists could _____ their movements and _____ their progress while they search for _____ of life. If one microbot gets lost, the mission could still continue.

A microbot attacking a cancer cell

5 **LEARN NEW WORDS Listen to these words and write them next to the definitions.** Then listen and repeat. ∩ 018 019

collaboration	co-ordinate	relief	situation	update

_____ 1. help for victims of a disaster

_____ 2. the process of working together

_____ 3. what is happening at a certain time and place

_____ 4. organise and connect people so they can work together

_____ 5. the latest information

6 **YOU DECIDE** **Choose an activity.**

1. **Work independently.** Write three survey questions about using technology to help crisis victims. Explain the idea of 'digital humanitarians' to several friends outside of class, and then ask them to answer your questions. Present their responses to the class.

2. **Work independently.** Interview a technology expert about how social media technology can be useful in helping people. You could interview a technology teacher at your school, a family member or another adult you know who works in technology. Present your interview in a magazine article.

3. **Work in groups.** Discuss ways that you can get crowdsourced information from the Internet.

Making suggestions	Agreeing	Disagreeing
I think _____ .	Great idea!	I see what you mean but _____ .
What if we _____ ?	I agree completely.	Wouldn't it be better if _____ ?
Wouldn't it be best to _____ ?	Sure, why not?	But don't you think _____ ?

1 **Listen.** How do the people make and respond to suggestions? Write the phrases you hear. 🎧021

2 **Read and complete the dialogue.**

Alan: Hey, Eva. Did you hear about the hurricane in the Caribbean? I've been busy helping out.

Eva: How can you help from far away?

Alan: I volunteer to read messages and look at photos from the area to decide who needs help.

Eva: _____ I wish there were something I could do.

Alan: _____ you should help out. _____ work together?

Eva: _____ I would need to be trained? I have no idea what to do!

Alan: I can show you. It's easy! And you could help a lot of people. What do you think?

Eva: _____

3 **Work in pairs.** Imagine there has been a natural disaster in another country. Student A spins the wheel and makes a suggestion how to help. Student B then spins the wheel to determine whether to agree or disagree. If Student B disagrees, he/she must make a new suggestion.

Go to page 153.

4 **Work in groups.** Talk about organising a fundraiser in your school to help victims of a natural disaster. Choose a cause and discuss ways to raise money for it. Make and respond to suggestions in your discussion.

GRAMMAR ∩ 022

Future tenses: Describing events in the future

Over the next few years, people **will look** online to find volunteers to help with disaster relief.

In the upcoming years, researchers **will be working** to develop new technologies that solve global problems.

By 2050, organisations **will have found** new online resources to solve their biggest problems.

1 **Listen.** Write the future tense forms you hear on the timeline. ∩ 023

In 2020, an 8.5 magnitude earthquake

_____

South America.

_____
_____
_____
_____

_____
_____
_____
_____

2020　　2030　　2040　　2050　　2060　　2070

By 2030, the world population

_____

around 8.3 billion people. World hunger levels

_____

By 2050, many regions in the world

_____

flooded because of rising sea levels.

Towards the end of the century, a massive asteroid

_____

the Earth's orbit.

2 **Work in pairs.** Make two additional predictions for the years 2040 and 2060. Write your answers in the spaces provided on the timeline from Activity 1.

3 **Work in groups.** Look again at predictions on the timeline. Discuss what scientists and everyday people will do to handle these situations. Use the future tenses in your answer.

> By 2050, scientists will have found better ways to predict the weather.

> And people will be preparing their homes for more hurricanes.

4 LEARN NEW WORDS **What can you do to help your neighbours?** Read the suggestions for helping in your own community. Then listen and repeat. 🎧024

What will you do the next time a disaster strikes? You know you can help others without ever leaving your home. But being involved in your community is also important. Over the next year, what will you be doing to help out locally?

Volunteer to clean up a beach or a local park.

Help out at a local library or animal shelter.

Hold a **fundraiser** to raise money for an important **cause**.

Organise and lead a **network** of young volunteers in your community.

5 **Listen.** Write the four activities mentioned in the dialogue. Then put a ✓ next to what the speakers decide to do as community service. 🎧025

_____

_____

_____

_____

6 **Work in pairs.** Brainstorm other ways to help individuals in your community. Include 1–2 examples that would require the use of technology. Which will you be doing? Why?

7 **Work in groups.** Join another pair and compare your ideas from Activity 6. Choose the best overall idea and create a radio or TV advert to encourage others to volunteer. Use future tenses to explain how the activity will benefit members of your community.

1 **BEFORE YOU READ Discuss in pairs.** Based on the title and the quotation, what do you think the reading is about?

2 **LEARN NEW WORDS Find these words in the reading.** What do you think they mean? Think about what type of word each one is. Then listen and repeat. 🎧 026

empower	engineer	face
generation	innovation	

3 **WHILE YOU READ Think about the title, the subtitle and the quotation.** 🎧 027

4 **AFTER YOU READ Work in pairs to answer the questions.**

1. What is a problem facing Sierra Leone?
2. What are two of Kelvin's inventions? How do they help others?
3. Why did David bring Kelvin to MIT for three weeks?
4. How does David work to promote innovation among young people?

FOCUS ON THE FUTURE

Kelvin Doe, also known as DJ Focus, is creating a future he wants to live in.

Imagine growing up in a place where the electricity is off more than it is on. Could you do anything to help your community? At 11 years old, Kelvin Doe saw the lack of power in his country, Sierra Leone, as a problem. Kelvin was committed to solving this problem, so he became an inventor.

Kelvin was forced to be creative in his inventions. He could not afford to buy supplies. So he collected broken electronic parts from the rubbish and taught himself how to engineer new devices. By 13, Kelvin was creating his own batteries by combining acid, soda and metal in tin cups. His simple invention gave light to a community often left in the dark, and it also led to other innovations.

At 14, Kelvin made his own FM radio transmitter and created his community's first local radio station. 'If we have a radio station,' he said, 'the people can debate issues affecting our community and Sierra Leone as a whole.' Kelvin, who took the name DJ Focus, quickly developed a group of loyal listeners.

Kelvin's hard work paid off. The national television station in Sierra Leone heard about his inventions and invited him to do a live demonstration on air. Shortly afterwards, he was invited to visit the Massachusetts Institute of Technology (MIT) to learn more about creative engineering. That visit was arranged by MIT doctoral student David Sengeh.

Like Kelvin, David grew up in Sierra Leone. He is a researcher at the MIT Media Lab, and founder of the organisation Global Minimum, Inc. Through this organisation, he aims to empower high school students in Sierra Leone by encouraging innovation. David wants more young Sierra Leoneans to be like Kelvin – to look at the problems their communities face and find ways to solve them so that their generation will have a better future.

Kelvin spent three weeks in the United States, learning from David and other researchers at MIT. At the end of the trip, he was ready to go home and get back to work. 'Whatever I've learnt here,' said Kelvin, 'I will share it with my friends, colleagues and loved ones, and do it as a team.'

'How do we create thousands of young people who are inspired by making stuff and solving the problems that are in their neighbourhood?'

David Sengeh, National Geographic Emerging Explorer, Biomedical Engineer

---

5　**Work in pairs.** Re-read the question in the quotation. Discuss why the question is important to David. Then try to answer it.

6　**Discuss in groups.**

1. What is a challenge facing your community? What could be done to solve it? What knowledge do you need to solve it?
2. How do David and Kelvin give back to the people of Sierra Leone? What can they learn from each other?
3. Re-read the following: *'Whatever I've learnt here, I will share it with my friends, colleagues and loved ones …'* What have you learnt that you can share with others? What can you accomplish when you share knowledge?

BEFORE YOU WATCH Work in pairs.
Summarise what you've learnt so far about crisis mapping. Who is involved? When is it needed? Who does it help?

Read and circle. The video you're going to watch is called *Crisis Mapping*. Think about what you've learnt in this unit and what you discussed in Activity 1. Then circle the words or phrases from the box that you think you'll hear in the video.

analyse data	digital	explore
police officers	silence	social media
helicopter	update	

WHILE YOU WATCH Outline the steps involved in crisis mapping. Watch scene 2.1.

AFTER YOU WATCH Work in pairs. Put the steps for crisis mapping in order.

_____ Digital humanitarians analyse data from the photos and text messages they receive.

_____ Thanks to the crisis maps, relief workers arrive at the locations where they're needed.

_____ People affected by the disaster take photos and send text messages.

_____ This data is used to generate crisis maps.

_____ A disaster, such as an earthquake or a cyclone, strikes.

_____ Relief workers analyse crisis maps.

A rescue worker provides water after an earthquake in Pakistan

5 **Work in pairs.** According to the video, what role does the TV news play during a crisis? Describe a time when you watched TV news to learn about a crisis. What was happening? What did you see and hear about on TV? How did you respond?

6 **Discuss in groups.** What skills do you have that would help you be an effective crisis mapper?

7 YOU DECIDE **Choose an activity.**

1. **Work independently.** Research the 2015 Nepal earthquake. What happened? Who helped? How? Write a news report to summarise the story.

2. **Work in pairs.** What is the difference between being a digital and a real-world humanitarian? List at least three differences. Is one more important than the other? More effective? Discuss your opinions.

3. **Work in groups.** At the end of the video, you're told to go online to learn more about crisis mapping organisations. Do this, and take notes on what you find. Prepare a short presentation for your classmates on organisations looking for digital humanitarians and what they need.

Quantifiers: Expressing amounts

Half of/Fifty per cent of the world's population **is** ...

The majority of/Most people are ...

A number of radio stations **are** online.

A lot of/Two-thirds of/Sixty-seven per cent of the people **are** ...

The majority of/Most of the population **is** ...

The number of radio stations worldwide **is** 51,000.

1 **Work independently.** Look at the graphic. Use the words below to summarise the information.

1. over half / population / every day

   <u>Over half of the world's population listens</u>
   <u>to the radio every day.</u>

2. majority / farmers / access to radio

   _____

   _____

3. a lot / young people / Internet

   _____

   _____

4. per cent / population / under 30

   _____

   _____

5. per cent / Africans / under 30

   _____

   _____

2 **Work in groups.** Make predictions about life in 20 years. Choose a topic and talk about it using an expression of quantity.

> In 20 years, 99 per cent of students will bring their own computers to school.

Go to page 157.

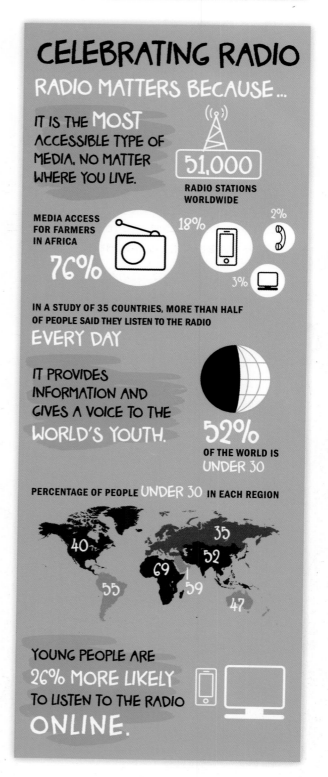

CELEBRATING RADIO

RADIO MATTERS BECAUSE ...

IT IS THE **MOST** ACCESSIBLE TYPE OF MEDIA, NO MATTER WHERE YOU LIVE.

51,000
RADIO STATIONS WORLDWIDE

MEDIA ACCESS FOR FARMERS IN AFRICA

76% 18% 2% 3%

IN A STUDY OF 35 COUNTRIES, MORE THAN HALF OF PEOPLE SAID THEY LISTEN TO THE RADIO **EVERY DAY**

IT PROVIDES INFORMATION AND GIVES A VOICE TO THE **WORLD'S YOUTH.**

52% OF THE WORLD IS UNDER 30

PERCENTAGE OF PEOPLE UNDER 30 IN EACH REGION

40 35 52 69 59 55 47

YOUNG PEOPLE ARE **26% MORE LIKELY** TO LISTEN TO THE RADIO **ONLINE.**

WRITING

In persuasive writing, you express your opinion or point of view about something important to you and support it, using phrases like:

based on

especially

equally important/necessary

It's clear that

1 **Read the model.** Work in pairs. How does the writer persuade the reader? Underline the words and phrases.

Did you know that 13th February is UNESCO's World Radio Day? On World Radio Day, UNESCO encourages young people to get involved with their local radio stations, get on the air and even create their own programmes. UNESCO believes it is especially important that there be more 'radio by youth, for youth'. This will help young people to get connected with one another and learn about the world around them.

More people have access to radio than to TV, computers or phones. A number of people can only get information on what is happening in the world from the radio. Equally important, there is almost no programming that targets young people, and yet we make up the majority of the population in many parts of the world.

Radio Tumaini, in Dar es Salaam, Tanzania, is one of the few stations that has a youth programme. Based on what workers and teen presenters say, the programme is a success. Young people are able to use radio to talk about topics that they care about, and listeners especially like hearing the teens talk about their experiences.

It's clear that we need to get involved in radio and make talk shows about issues that are important to us. Let's become reporters and tell the stories we think are important. There is an audience out there, waiting to hear what we have to say.

2 **Work in pairs.** Look again at the graphic on page 36. What other persuasive information about youth and radio could the writer have included in this paragraph?

3 **Write.** Persuade your readers to take part in a local or global community service project.

NATIONAL GEOGRAPHIC

Do Your Part

'We're proving what can happen when ordinary people collaborate and use technology to make a positive, lifesaving difference.'

Patrick Meier
National Geographic Explorer, Crisis Mapper

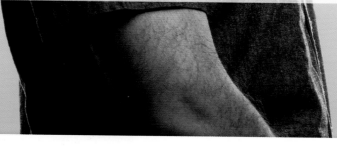

1. **Watch scene 2.2.**

2. Have you ever used technology to help others? Does technology make it more likely that you will do your part when there's a natural disaster? Explain.

3. Patrick Meier uses technology to bring people together from all over the world. How are you using technology now to connect with people around the world? How do you think this will change in the future?

Make an Impact

YOU DECIDE Choose a project.

1 **Raise awareness for charity.**

· Research a local or international charity.
· Create a presentation about the charity's mission.
· Present your work to the class.

2 **Discover a teen inventor.**

· Choose a teenage inventor who has made something to help others.
· Research their invention and how they made it. Create a drawing of it.
· Explain the invention to the class.

3 **Invent a solution yourself.**

· Think of a problem that affects a lot of people.
· Design a technological gadget that could solve this problem.
· Explain to the class how your gadget works.

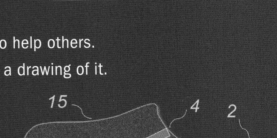

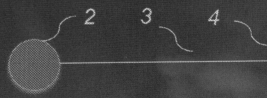

Teen inventor Kenneth Shinozuka invented a device to help his grandfather, who suffers from Alzheimer's disease.

Express Yourself

1 Read and listen to *The Adventures of Crisis Crusher.* 🎧 029

2 Discuss in groups.

1. What happens in the comic strip?

2. What obstacles do the characters have to overcome?

3. Why does Crisis Crusher need the help of others? How do the people

3 **Connect ideas.** In Unit 1, you learnt how people push physical and mental limits to achieve their personal goals. In Unit 2, you learnt about people working together for a common goal. In both cases, people overcome obstacles for a purpose. What does this tell you about yourself? What can you accomplish by yourself? What can you accomplish with the help of others?

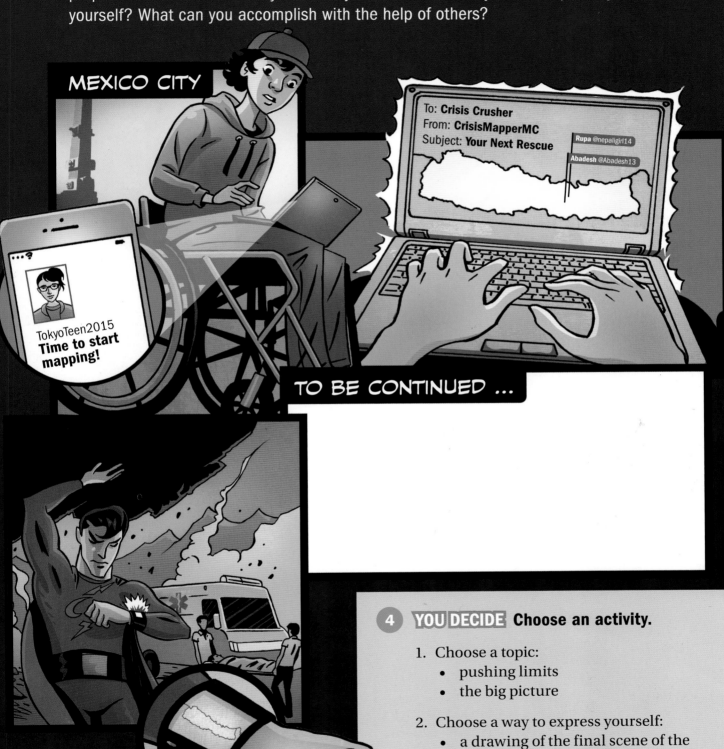

4 **YOU DECIDE** **Choose an activity.**

1. Choose a topic:
   - pushing limits
   - the big picture

2. Choose a way to express yourself:
   - a drawing of the final scene of the Crisis Crusher story
   - a written ending to Crisis Crusher's story
   - a theme song for Crisis Crusher

3. Present your work.

Food Matters

An Alaskan woman kissing a sockeye salmon that she caught

'As an act of exploration, taste your world.'
Barton Seaver

TO START

1. Why do you think this woman is kissing a fish?

2. Why is food important for your health? For your culture? Explain.

3. What are some of your favourite foods? Where do you get these foods?

1 **Where does our food come from? Why does it matter?** Discuss. Then listen and read. 🎧 **030**

What did you eat for breakfast this morning? For dinner last night? You might have mealtime routines that are the same – or almost the same – each day. But did you ever stop and think about the connection you have to food?

In the past, people often grew their own crops and raised their own animals. Once the food was **harvested**, they worked together to get the food to the table. This collaboration helped people to connect with one another, and with the food they prepared.

Harvesting food

Chef and **conservationist** Barton Seaver realised at a young age that food is part of the human experience. As a child, Barton lived in a **diverse** community. Immigrants who lived there brought foods from their cultures with them. Barton's parents cooked with these foods, and Barton was grateful to be able to explore the world right from his kitchen. He learnt that food is a **reflection** of culture: it's part of who we are.

Today, this connection between food and people is breaking down. **Globalisation** allows food to be shipped anywhere in the world. Since you can buy

Modern industrial farming

according to your **tastes**, there's no need to wait until foods become available. And you don't have to spend hours preparing meals as a family. Foods have been prepared and **packaged** to be more **convenient**. Although they make life easier, these foods are not as **wholesome** as fresh, **local** foods. Packaging and transporting foods also **impacts** on the environment.

Barton studies the effects of our food choices on the environment, especially the oceans. He understands that we have preferences about seafood, and that fishermen try to get us what we want. But **commercial** fishing has upset the ocean's ecosystem, and Barton is working to help people change their attitudes about food so that they make better choices.

So, the next time you sit down to a nice main course of fish and vegetables, think about what you're eating. Are the vegetables from a nearby farm or from across the world? Is the fish on your plate an overfished species? Enjoy your dinner, but don't ignore where it comes from. Remember, your choices count!

2 **LEARN NEW WORDS Listen and repeat.** 🎧 031

3 **Work in pairs.** Describe what you ate and drank at your last meal. Was it wholesome? Where do you think this meal came from? What impact do you think it had on the environment?

4 **Read and write the words from the list.** Make any necessary changes.

commercial	diverse	globalisation	harvest	impact
local	packaged	reflection	taste	wholesome

According to Barton, food is a _____ of our culture. He should know. Barton grew up in a very _____ community, where he learnt about different cultures through food. Barton sees food as a way to connect with people we know and people we don't know. Trying new foods can _____ our relationship with people and help us understand other cultures. Barton also sees _____ foods as the best choice. Choosing from what's produced nearby makes us try new things, not just buy according to our _____ . Although _____ farming and fishing offer a wide variety of foods in the supermarket, Barton wants us to avoid popular, overfished species, and instead try the 'catch of the day'. We should get creative with what is available to create unique, _____ meals.

5 **LEARN NEW WORDS Listen to these words and then match them to the correct definition.** Then listen and repeat. 🎧 **032 033**

attitude	grateful	main course
_____		1. feeling or opinion
_____		2. main part of a meal
_____		3. thankful

Commercial fishing

6 **YOU DECIDE Choose an activity.**

1. **Work independently.** Think about the food produced in your region and plan a main course that uses local ingredients. Present your meal idea to the class.
2. **Work in pairs.** Discuss what affects your food choices more: your own tastes or what foods are available to you. Do you make good food choices? Explain.
3. **Work in groups.** Create a survey of food awareness. Work together to write five questions about food. Conduct the survey in class. Then present the results.

SPEAKING STRATEGY 🎧034

Offering advice	Accepting or declining advice
You should think about <u>helping us in the community garden.</u>	Actually, I was thinking <u>we could work in the school's garden.</u>
If I were you, I'd <u>sign up for the school's gardening club.</u>	Great idea! Thanks for the suggestion!
Why don't you try <u>growing vegetables at home?</u>	Thanks for the idea, but I <u>prefer working in my grandfather's garden.</u>

1 **Listen.** How do the speakers offer and respond to advice? Write the words and phrases you hear. 🎧035

2 **Read and complete the dialogue.**

Natalia: I'm so tired of eating the same old thing.

Alex: _____ eating something different? What foods do you like?

Natalia: Well, I love chicken, bread, rice …

Alex: _____ , I'd look for dishes from other cultures with those ingredients. Have you tried Indian food?

Natalia: No. _____ , but I don't eat spicy foods.

Alex: Not all Indian food is spicy. And many Indian dishes use chicken and rice. Indian bread, called *naan*, is really delicious, too!

Natalia: Really?

Alex: Really! _____ you could come over and try some Indian food at my house. My dad's making it tomorrow night.

Natalia: _____

3 **Work in groups.** Spin the wheel. Give advice on the topic. Listen as group members respond to your advice.

> You should think about trying sardines. They're really good!

Go to page 157.

4 **Work in pairs.** You want to eat more responsibly. Listen and respond to your partner's advice on how to do so.

Mixed conditionals: Expressing how things would be different

If I **hadn't learnt** about overfishing, **I would** still **be eating** tuna.

If you **had learnt** about Indian food sooner, **you wouldn't** still **be eating** pizza all the time.

1 **Read.** Circle the correct answer.

1. If I *had learnt / learnt* how to cook, I *wouldn't be / wouldn't have been* eating sandwiches all the time.

2. I *wouldn't have been / wouldn't be* eating chips now, if I *had remembered / remembered* to pack my lunch.

3. What *would we call / would we have called* a sandwich today if the Earl of Sandwich *didn't ask / hadn't asked* for his food to be served between two pieces of toast?

2 **Listen.** Complete the sentences. 🎧037

1. If Barton Seaver hadn't grown up in a family where trying different foods was so important, _____

    _____ .

2. _____ ,
    we would still be more closely connected to what we eat.

3. If we had stayed more connected to our food, _____

    _____ .

3 **Work in pairs.** Talk about what would be different now in these situations.

1. If I had never tried (food), ...

2. If I had (never) learnt to cook, ...

3. If I hadn't learnt about food awareness, ...

> If I had learnt to cook when I was younger, I wouldn't be eating so much packaged food.

> Yes, and if I hadn't learnt about food awareness, I wouldn't read labels carefully.

4 LEARN NEW WORDS Listen and read about food revolutionaries. Then listen and repeat. 🎧 038 039

Barton Seaver

Christopher Columbus (1451–1506)

Auguste Escoffier (1846–1935)

You have already learnt that Barton Seaver is a food **revolutionary**. He wants to change the way we eat, especially seafood. According to Barton, if we hadn't overfished popular fish like tuna and cod, the ocean's ecosystem wouldn't be out of balance. Barton understands that fish is in demand because it's a healthy source of **protein**. He just wants people to try fish that are lower on the food chain. This would help **restore** the population of overfished species. Barton is trying to make changes today, but there were other food revolutionaries long before him.

Christopher Columbus is known around the world as an explorer. But Columbus is also one of the first food revolutionaries. If he hadn't travelled west in search of **spices** from India, he would never have arrived in the Americas. And if he and other explorers hadn't arrived in the Americas, foods such as tomatoes, potatoes, corn and cacao would not have been brought back to Europe. Without Columbus's exploration, the modern diet of many cultures would be much different.

Another food revolutionary is French chef Auguste Escoffier. Escoffier wanted to make the process of cooking more standard. He wrote down ingredients and necessary steps for each of his dishes. If Escoffier hadn't done this, we might not have **recipes** or cookbooks!

5 Work in pairs. Talk about how things would be if it weren't for food revolutionaries. Used mixed conditionals in your discussion, as well as the words from the box.

corn	fish	potato	recipe	spice	write

6 Work independently. Research another food revolutionary, such as Julia Child, Clarence Birdseye or Ettore Bioardi. Write about the person you chose. Say how things would be different if it hadn't been for that person's work. Present your research to the class.

Tomatoes and corn were brought to Europe from the Americas in the 1500s.

1 **BEFORE YOU READ Discuss in pairs.** Based on what you have learnt so far and the photo on this page, what do you think the reading is about?

2 **LEARN NEW WORDS Find these words in the reading.** What do you think they mean? Think about the context of this unit. Then listen and repeat. 🎧 040

consistent	organic
sustainable	vertical

3 **WHILE YOU READ Think about how what you have learnt so far in this unit relates to the text.** 🎧 041

National Geographic Explorer Caleb Harper and his CityFarm

Grow IT HERE, Eat IT HERE

With 80 per cent of the world's population living in cities by the year 2050, we need to consider indoor farming.

What do you think of when you hear the word *farm*? You probably think of a large, open space with lots of different crops growing and animals grazing, don't you? Well, urban agriculturalist Caleb Harper is working to

Over the past few years, Caleb has been researching different forms of vertical farming. He has been working to bring farms into the city. His main focus is on two types of vertical farming: *aeroponics* and *hydroponics*. With aeroponics, a nutrient-filled mist is sprayed on a plant's roots to help them grow without soil. With hydroponics, a plant is grown in nutrient-rich water.

Caleb uses simple computer technologies to monitor his crops. This technology allows him to control climate and provide consistent light, food, temperature and water. The result is better plant growth and flavour. This consistency also allows his crops to produce food four to five times faster than those of a traditional outdoor farmer.

Caleb's work is important. At the moment, we are facing a global food crisis. The world's population is at seven billion. In 30 years, it will be nearly nine billion. We will need to produce 70 per cent more food to feed these additional people, but there isn't enough farmland.

CITY FARM

Even if there were, traditional farming can be harmful to land. Over-used soil loses nutrients. Farmers use chemicals to treat their crops. These chemicals get into the ground and run off into bodies of water. The polluted water supply threatens the ecosystem and the health of those living nearby.

Vertical farming systems can help solve these problems. First, farms in urban areas will allow people to harvest fresh produce year-round. There is no need to worry about threats such as droughts or insects, which could ruin a crop. And indoor farms are sustainable. They use less water than a traditional farm, and with aeroponics, 97 per cent of fresh water is re-used. Vertical farms use less energy because they don't depend on large farming equipment and long transportation systems to carry the food from farm to city. And all of the crops in an indoor farm are grown without pesticides, so they are fresh, healthy and organic.

So, the next time you hear the word *farm*, don't just think of that large, open space with crops and animals. Think inside the city – it's the future of farming.

4 **AFTER YOU READ** Work in pairs to answer the questions.

1. Describe Caleb Harper's indoor farm.
2. Why is Caleb's work important?
3. What are *aeroponics* and *hydroponics*?
4. What are two problems with traditional farming?
5. What are three ways that indoor farms are sustainable?

5 **Work in groups.** Using what you have learnt in the unit, discuss whether you think Barton Seaver would support Caleb's work. Give examples to support your ideas.

6 **Discuss in groups.**

1. Vertical farms will help provide food for our growing population. What is another way we can produce more food?
2. Apart from the health and environmental benefits, what other benefits could indoor farming bring to a city?

VIDEO ▶

1 **BEFORE YOU WATCH** **Discuss in groups.**

   1. What is the most unusual food you have ever eaten? Why did you try it? Did you like it?

   2. Look at the photo of *chapulines*. This dish is eaten in parts of Mexico. Have you ever tried this dish, or a similar one? Would you try it? Why or why not?

2 **Work in pairs.** The video presents problems related to food and how eating insects might solve those problems. Predict a problem and a solution that the video may mention. Write your answers in the space below.

Problem	Solution
_____	_____
_____	_____
_____	_____

3 **WHILE YOU WATCH** **Check your predictions from Activity 2.** Watch scene 3.1.

A grasshopper

4 **Read the sentences below.** Use the information from the video to decide if each one is *true* or *false*.

1. Presently, very few people in the world eat insects. (T) (F)

2. Beetles and caterpillars are the insects most commonly eaten by people. (T) (F)

3. There are fewer than 200 species of edible insects. (T) (F)

4. Insects are a good solution to the increased demand for protein. (T) (F)

5. Insects are already being used to produce food for farm animals. (T) (F)

6. Eating insects is really harmful for the environment. (T) (F)

5 **Work in pairs.** This video suggests that we try something new, even if it seems unpleasant. Think about a time when you had to try a new dish, even though you didn't want to. Who or what made you try it? Was it what you expected? Explain.

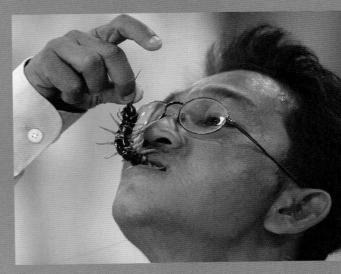

Eating a centipede

6 **YOU DECIDE** **Choose an activity.**

1. **Work independently.** Find out about another unusual food source that people may not want to eat, such as snake meat or snails. Learn about where this food is eaten, who eats it and how it is prepared. Write a paragraph to summarise what you learnt.

2. **Work in pairs.** Make a list of six things that people would consider unpleasant to eat, such as insects, worms or certain animal parts. Survey ten people to find out which of these things they are most likely to try, and which they wouldn't try. Present your survey results to the class.

3. **Work in groups.** Prepare a radio advert to convince listeners to try eating insects. In your advert, explain at least three benefits of eating insects.

GRAMMAR 🎧042

Double comparatives: Describing outcomes

The more people there are in the world, **the more** food we need to produce.

The less our food travels, **the less** it impacts the environment.

The more we choose wholesome foods, **the healthier** we are.

The less we eat processed foods, **the better**.

1 **Complete the sentences with comparative phrases.**

1. The more new foods we try, _____ .

2. The less time we spend cooking, _____ .

3. The more we know about food, _____ .

4. The less we waste food, _____ .

5. The more indoor farms there are, _____ .

6. The higher the population, _____ .

7. The less we use chemicals, _____ .

8. The more seafood we demand, _____ .

2 **Work in pairs.** Discuss two ways that food choices impact the environment. Use comparative sentences in your discussion.

> The more we ship food across the world, the more we impact the environment.

> That's right! And the more we buy from local farms, the less we impact the environment.

3 **Work in groups.** Take a card. Use a comparative sentence to comment on the topic. Then discuss the comment. Each group member should agree or disagree with the comment.

share with others

Go to page 159.

WRITING

When you write a review, you combine facts and opinions to describe a place (such as a hotel or a restaurant) or a thing (such as a book, a song or a film). Use the following words to show your attitude when writing a review:

actually   **clearly**   **honestly**   **more/most importantly**   **(un)fortunately**

1 **Read the model.** Work in pairs to identify the facts and the author's opinions about the restaurant. What words does the writer use when showing his/her attitude about the restaurant? Underline the words.

If you are looking for a great meal, you should really go to Jozsa's Restaurant. The more I eat there, the better it gets. I'm not the only one who thinks that Jozsa's has the best food in town: the restaurant has actually won many awards for its excellent dishes, such as roasted chicken with potatoes, and beef with noodles. The fish main courses are all delicious as well. Everything at this restaurant is worth a try. And don't forget to save room for dessert. Honestly, the chocolate cake is the best you'll ever have!

Clearly, the chef at this restaurant uses fresh ingredients. There is a large garden behind the restaurant where they grow vegetables and herbs that are used in the dishes. Nothing on the menu is made with packaged foods. For this reason, I feel like Jozsa's is a great choice for a wholesome meal if you can't cook at home.

Fortunately, Jozsa's is open every night from 5.00 to 11.00, and for lunch at the weekends. The restaurant is very busy, so you will want to make a reservation. The service is fantastic every time! The workers are friendly, and more importantly, they always have the food on your table quickly. The inside and outside of the restaurant are both great places to eat. If it's cold outside, try to get a seat next to the fireplace. In nice weather, you can enjoy your dinner in the garden.

Every time my family has something to celebrate, we choose Jozsa's. If you haven't tried Jozsa's yet, you don't know what you're missing!

2 **Work in pairs.** Does this review convince you to try this restaurant? Why or why not?

3 **Write.** Write a review about your favourite restaurant. Give both facts and opinions of the food, the service and the surroundings.

Know Your Food

'Take some time to educate yourself about the right decisions – and make a difference in the health of the planet.'

Barton Seaver

National Geographic Explorer, Chef/Conservationist

1. **Watch scene 3.2.**

2. How much do you know about the food that you eat each day? Why is it important to be informed about food choices?

3. What steps can you take to learn more about the food you eat? Name at least two things you can do to be better informed.

Make an Impact

YOU DECIDE Choose a project.

1 **Create a sustainable lunch menu.**

· List food groups that you would include on a lunch menu.

· Research sustainable options for each of these food groups.

· Create a lunch menu for a week that includes wholesome foods that don't negatively impact the environment.

2 **Profile a well-known chef.**

· Research a chef who works to create sustainable dishes.

· Write a biography of the chef, including information on how he or she connects with food. Include one of the chef's recipes in your profile.

· Present your research to the class.

3 **Plan and host a cooking show.**

· Research sustainable, wholesome meals. Choose a dish to feature on your show.

· Choose ingredients for your dish. Describe the ingredients that you chose and why they are good choices.

· Using the ingredients, demonstrate how to prepare the dish. Explain the process.

The Footprint of Fun

'An individual action, multiplied by millions, creates global change.'
Jack Johnson

Japanese fans wave rubbish bags before cleaning up after a World Cup game.

TO START

1. When you attend a sporting event, do you clean up after yourself? Why or why not?

2. What fun things can you think of that might not be good for the environment? Which of them do you do?

3. What do you like to do for fun that doesn't harm the environment?

Tivoli Gardens in Copenhagen, Denmark

Your last visit to an **amusement** park was probably pretty **enjoyable**, wasn't it? **Attractions** such as rides, shows and games are really fun for visitors. While you're on a roller coaster or playing games in the arcade, you probably don't consider your environmental impact.

Think about it: amusement parks **consume** huge amounts of energy. Just going up the hill of one roller coaster ride uses enough energy to power a lamp for over 30 hours. Some high-speed rides use enough energy to power a small town. Amusement parks also use **excessive** amounts of water in rides, fountains and other park **facilities**. And then there is the issue of rubbish. Tonnes of **litter** are being produced in amusement parks by the millions of people who visit. Disneyland alone produces over 270,000 tonnes of litter each year, more than a mid-sized city!

Parks such as Ancol Dreamland in Jakarta, Indonesia, have recycling programmes for visitors.

Conservation is nothing new for the **industry**. Walt Disney thought about it back in 1955 while designing his first park, Disneyland California. Disney himself planned for the use of recycled water throughout his park. Even today, employees of Disney's parks are proactive in keeping them sustainable. At Disneyland Hong Kong, run-off rainwater is being collected into a lake and then re-used throughout the resort. And Disney parks are designed to be clean, with litter bins located every 30 steps inside the park. Each one leads to an underground system where rubbish is pushed through pipes at over 95 kph. (60 mph.) and ultimately compacted. Disney is also taking action to prevent waste. By using recyclable materials and **composting**, the parks have reduced litter by over 60 per cent.

Other parks are also becoming **sensitive** to their environmental impact. They are starting to **participate** in the green **movement** with positive **results**. Park vehicles and trains at the US-based Six Flags now run on used vegetable oil from the parks' kitchens. Copenhagen's Tivoli Gardens, one of the oldest amusement parks in the world, has a windmill that generates all its electricity.

These changes produce both environmental and **economic** benefits. As sustainable ideas and technology become more **accessible**, it's easier than ever for amusement parks to be green!

2 **LEARN NEW WORDS Listen and repeat.** 🎧044

3 **Work in pairs.** Describe a recent trip to an amusement park or a public event. Did you see any litter there? Was there an effort to recycle? What else was being done to protect the environment?

4 Read and write the words from the list. Make any necessary changes.

| accessible | consume | economic | enjoyable | excessive |
| industry | litter | participate | result | sensitive |

It's good to know that the music _____ has environmental champions like Jack Johnson. Jack is a singer and surfer who is very _____ about nature. He was concerned about the negative impact his concert tours were having on the environment. So he decided to cut out _____ waste and _____ less energy. The _____ of that decision is that Jack now fuels his tour buses with biofuel, and performs at places that are _____ by public transport. He also invites non-profit-making organisations to _____ in educating fans about sustainability at his concert venues.

Jack
Johnson

5 LEARN NEW WORDS Listen to these words and match them to the definitions. Then listen and repeat. ⌂ 045 046

| benefit | non-profit | proactive | take action |

_____ 1. a positive effect

_____ 2. preparing for possible future problems

_____ 3. do something about a problem

_____ 4. not focused on making money

6 YOU DECIDE Choose an activity.

1. **Work independently.** Research what another well-known person or organisation is doing for the environment. Share what you learnt with the class.

2. **Work in pairs.** Keep a journal of what you throw away in a day. Compare with your partner. How much waste did you produce? How can you reduce the amount of waste you produce?

3. **Work in groups.** Do you think musicians should be responsible for making their events more environmentally friendly? What can they say or do to make their fans more proactive in protecting the planet? Discuss. Then list three suggestions.

Defending your opinion

I heard that <u>racing cars use a lot of fuel</u>.

I read that <u>they use around 20,000 litres (5,300 gal.) in a race</u>.

Most people would agree that <u>there are greener forms of entertainment</u>.

As far as I know, <u>these industries are trying to go green</u>.

All I'm saying is <u>that electric cars and aeroplanes will change the industry</u>.

1 **Listen.** How do the speakers defend their opinions? Write the phrases you hear. 048

2 **Read and complete the dialogue.**

Jacob: Hey, Lily. My family and I are going to the air show on Saturday. Would you like to join us?

Lily: Well, air shows are a little too noisy for me. _____ they're really bad for the environment, too.

Jacob: Well, it's true that air shows do consume a lot of fuel. But, _____ , the industry is developing new, more efficient planes. _____ an electric plane might fly all the way around the world.

Lily: OK, but the planes at the show won't be electric. Those planes burn a lot of fuel *and* blow smoke into the environment. _____ they have a huge environmental impact.

Jacob: Actually, _____ the coloured smoke is biodegradable and doesn't harm the environment.

Lily: Well, the fuel that's burnt certainly does. Sorry, Jacob. I hope you have fun, but I would rather not come. Let's get together on Sunday instead. You can tell me all about the show.

3 **Work in pairs.** Take turns giving and defending your opinion using the information on the cards.

4 **Work in groups.** Discuss the information on the cards again. This time, express your own opinion.

Buying bottled water isn't bad for the environment. You just need to recycle the bottles.

Really? I've heard that only one in five bottles actually gets recycled.

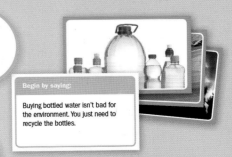

Begin by saying:

Buying bottled water isn't bad for the environment. You just need to recycle the bottles.

Go to page 161.

Passives: Describing actions and processes

What have musicians done to reduce their ecological footprint?

What **has been done** by musicians to reduce their ecological footprint?

Jack Johnson's music is promoting sustainability.

Sustainability **is being promoted** through Jack Johnson's music.

Jack can teach his fans about conservation. They will pass on the ideas to their friends.

Jack's fans **can be taught** about conservation. The ideas **will be passed on** to friends.

1 **Read the information in the graphic.** Underline the examples of the passive.

2 **Listen.** Complete the sentences. ∩ 050

So you _____ that some fun activities can harm the environment. But Jack Johnson is working towards his goal that the environment _____ by his concerts. Water refill stations _____ throughout his concert venues. Fans _____ to bring their own reusable water bottles. And Jack's team works together with farms to make sure that sustainable food _____ . Jack hopes that his message is coming through, and that his fans _____ by their experience at his show.

3 **Work in groups.** Talk about environmental improvements to your school or city. What has been done to protect the environment? What was done recently? What else can be done? What do you think will be done in the near future? Use the passive in your discussion.

200 BILLION LITRES (44 billion gal.) of bottled water are being consumed worldwide every year.

More than **40%** of all bottled water is being produced from **TAP WATER.**

Bottled water can be sold at nearly **10,000** TIMES the price of tap water.

Bottled water has **NOT** been found to be **SAFER** than tap water.

Almost **1/4** of bottled water has been **CONTAMINATED.**

Only **1** IN **5** water bottles is being recycled.

More than **1** MILLION TONNES (2.2 BILLION LB.) of waste will be produced from the other four bottles.

4 **LEARN NEW WORDS** **Read about the effects of plastic on the environment and what you can do about it.** Then listen and repeat. 🎧 051 052

Recently, the worldwide **demand** for plastic has exploded. Plastic is all around us – our gadgets, dishes, furniture – almost everything is made of plastic these days! Plastic is convenient, but most of us never think about the **damage** caused by using too much plastic.

Jack says, '**Challenge** yourself to reduce your plastic footprint.'

Why should we do this? And how can we?

Litter from plastic products dirties our cities. Much of the plastic ends up in landfill, where it can last up to 500 years! But worse is that our oceans are being polluted by plastics. There are around eight million tonnes of plastic **waste** in the world's oceans. Over 700 species of marine wildlife have been **harmed** by this pollution. Many animals mistake plastic for food. Over 100,000 marine animals die each year from eating plastic. Others might survive, but some of them end up on our plates. So, humans are also being harmed by plastic in the oceans.

To make a positive change, we can:

• Reduce the amount of plastic we use each day.

• Re-use by carrying our own water bottles and bags.

• Recycle any additional plastic we use.

Whether you're going to school, to the park or to a concert, think about your footprint.

A sea turtle tries to eat a plastic bag that it has mistaken for a jellyfish.

5 **Work in pairs.** Think about Jack's message. Write five things that can be done to reduce the use of plastic in your daily life. Use the passive.

6 **Work in groups.** Research how bottled water consumption and recycling have changed over the years. Present what you learnt to the class, using the passive.

Ten per cent more bottled water is being consumed each year.

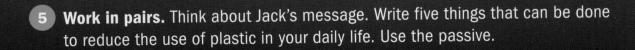

1 **BEFORE YOU READ Discuss in pairs.**
Based on what you have learnt so far in this unit and the photos on this page, what do you think the reading is about?

2 **LEARN NEW WORDS Find these words in the reading.** What do you think they mean? Use the other words in the sentence to help you. Then listen and repeat. 🎧 053

> cost   development   maintain   venue

3 **WHILE YOU READ Think about the author's purpose.** 🎧 054

4 **AFTER YOU READ Work in pairs to answer the questions.**

1. What is a benefit of hosting the Olympics?

2. What are two negative results of hosting the Olympics?

3. What was the total cost of the 2004 Summer Olympics?

4. Give an example of how an Olympic site is being re-used.

5. What should Olympic host cities do to avoid ending up with a 'ghost town'?

GAME OVER

After the torch goes out, what happens to Olympic sites?

How would you feel if your city were chosen to host the Olympic Games? The best athletes in the world would be right outside your door! The games bring excitement and attention to your region, as well as a lot of development. But the Olympics also have great economic and environmental costs. People have even been forced to leave their homes to make way for the Olympics. And once the last medal is awarded and the athletes have gone home, you may be left with a ghost town.

Greece is the birthplace of the Olympics. So the country was excited to welcome the 2004 Summer Olympics back to Athens.

An abandoned Olympic training pool in Athens, Greece

After years of preparation, and nearly U.S. $11 billion spent, the athletes arrived, and the games began. The 2004 Summer Olympics were a success. But shortly after they ended, the venues began to fall apart. Most of them sit empty today. The Olympic training pool is used by frogs, not athletes. Until recently, the Greek government was still paying to maintain these buildings, bringing the total cost of the 2004 Summer Olympics to over U.S. $50 billion. Athens isn't alone. Many Olympic sites have become ghost towns. The abandoned site of the 1936 Summer Olympics is still standing in Berlin, nearly a century after it was built.

With good planning, Olympic venues can be successfully re-used. In many cities, former Olympic stadiums continue to host sporting events. Barcelona, host of the 1992 Summer Olympics, has been creative in re-using its venues. Barcelona's Port Olímpic, built for the Olympic sailing competition, is now a popular tourist destination, with a museum, hotels, shops and restaurants. Tourists visiting Beijing can now enjoy a water park experience at the Water Cube, where swimming records were broken during the 2008 Summer Olympics.

Hosting the Olympic Games is an honour. But the games only last 17 days! Olympic venues shouldn't simply be designed to be used for a couple of weeks. These facilities can improve a region only when they're designed for the long-term benefit of everyone. Architects who create quality facilities that serve a community for the years after the Olympics deserve a gold medal!

The Water Cube in Beijing, China

5 **Work in pairs.** Think about the information in the reading. Why do you think the author wrote this text? What is the author's message?

6 **Discuss in groups.**

1. Would you like the Olympics to come to your country? Why or why not?

2. Imagine your city or town has been chosen to host the Olympic Games. What needs to be built? How will your city change?

3. What could the International Olympic Committee do to make sure that the venues designed for the Olympic Games don't turn into 'ghost towns'? Give two or three examples.

VIDEO ▶

1 **BEFORE YOU WATCH Discuss in groups.**
Describe the size and the atmosphere of a concert or big sporting event that you've attended.

2 **Discuss in groups.** You're going to watch a video called *The Footprint of Fans*. Based on what you have learnt so far in this unit, predict three ways fans leave an ecological footprint when they attend an event.

3 **WHILE YOU WATCH Fill in a T-chart.** List two problems and two solutions mentioned in the video. **Watch scene 4.1.**

4 **AFTER YOU WATCH Complete the sentences below.**

1. Fans are responsible for up to
   _____ of a concert's carbon footprint.

2. Some concert venues reward fans who carpool by giving them _____ .

3. Some sporting events can fill a stadium with up to _____ fans.

4. Sports fans can leave behind
   _____ tonnes of waste.

5. Recycled plastic and other materials are now used to make _____ .

Fans at the closing ceremony for the 2015 European Games held in Baku, Azerbaijan

5 **Work in pairs.** Tick the ways the video suggests that we can reduce our fan footprint.

- [ ] only watch games on TV
- [ ] carpool to concerts
- [ ] buy recycled sporting equipment
- [ ] pay less money for tickets
- [ ] recycle water bottles
- [ ] go to fewer concerts and sporting events

6 **Discuss in groups.** Answer the questions you see at the end of the video: *What else are you a fan of? How does it impact the environment? How can you take action to become an eco-friendly fan?*

7 **YOU DECIDE** **Choose an activity.**

1. **Work independently.** Research a concert or sporting event. How could the organisers have made the event greener? Write a letter to the organisers presenting at least three ideas.

2. **Work in pairs.** Survey your classmates to find out how many attend big events such as concerts or sporting events. Create five questions about transport, rubbish, energy use and recycling at these events. Summarise and report your findings.

3. **Work in groups.** Make a short presentation to your local politicians suggesting how to reduce the carbon footprint of big events in your city.

Verbs followed by gerunds or infinitives

Most water parks **want to use less** water.

How can they **avoid wasting** water?

Park employees **encourage** visitors **to keep** water inside the pool.

Maybe parks should just **stop using** so much water.

We should **stop to look at** the root of the problem.

Parks must **continue coming up with /** **to come up with** ways to re-use water.

1 **Work independently.** Complete the sentences with the correct form of the verb in brackets. Go to page 152.

1. This summer, I hope _____ (visit) my favourite water park.

2. Although I can't wait _____ (play) in the water each summer, I agree that parks should start _____ (conserve) more water.

3. Park designers should continue _____ (think) of new ways to use less water.

4. Park operators shouldn't stop _____ (clean) and _____ (re-use) the water in their attractions.

5. Some parks even choose _____ (collect) rainwater for use in their attractions.

6. Of course, if you want _____ (enjoy) water in a way that doesn't harm the environment, consider _____ (go) to the beach!

2 **Work in pairs.** Your school wants students to conserve water. Make a list of five suggestions. Use some of the verbs below followed by an infinitive or a gerund.

ask	avoid	choose	continue	start	stop	tell	want

3 **Work in groups.** You are planning an event to raise awareness for the environment. Throw a coin and take turns moving (heads = 1 space; tails = 2 spaces). Say what you need to do.

We should think about finding a venue that's accessible by bus.

START

Find a venue that's accessible by bus. (think about)

Advertise with social media, not paper. (continue)

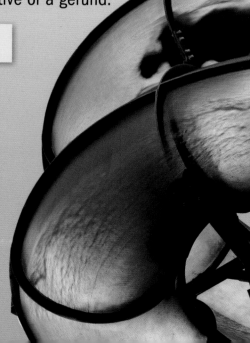

Go to page 163.

WRITING

When writing a problem and solution essay, focus on including both information and reflection. Information can be provided about a problem, and reflection on the problem can lead to solutions. When writing about problems and solutions, the following phrases are useful:

Problem:	**due to**	**it's true that**	**the issue is**
Solution:	**in order to**	**one solution is**	**will result in**

1 **Read the model.** What is the problem? Underline the phrases that help you find it.

I love going to water parks for fun. However, many people think that water parks are bad for the environment. The issue is that the parks waste water. Due to a lack of drinking water in many parts of the world, people think water shouldn't be used just to have fun. It's true that thousands of litres of water are used every day at a single water park. And there are nearly 2,000 water parks around the world, so that's a lot of water!

Water park operators understand that they need to conserve water, especially in places with dry climates. One solution that has been developed is to recycle water. Using special filters, water parks are able to clean and re-use most of the water in their facilities. Some indoor water parks are able to recycle as much as 97 per cent of the water they use. Outdoor water parks lose water because of the sun. Building attractions in the shade will result in less water being lost. All water parks lose water when visitors splash it out of the pool. So, new designs are being created in order to keep water in the pools and prevent it from being wasted.

Water parks attract millions of people each year, so they aren't going away any time soon. If you think water is wasted at water parks, think about how much more water would be used if each visitor instead cooled off with a pool or a sprinkler at home! In that case, you could argue that water parks actually help conserve water.

2 **Work in pairs.** How many solutions did the writer give to the problem? What were they? Think of another solution to the problem.

3 **Write.** Think about an activity that you enjoy that may be harmful to the environment. Write an essay to describe why it's a problem. Give at least three possible solutions to the problem.

NATIONAL GEOGRAPHIC

Reduce Your Footprint

'Your actions, your voice and your choices
all have a huge impact.'

Jack Johnson
National Geographic Ambassador to the Arts, Musician

1. **Watch scene 4.2.**

2. Are you aware of how your actions affect the environment? What are some things you could do to further reduce your footprint?

3. What advice could you offer to friends and family for having fun without harming the environment?

Make an Impact

YOU DECIDE Choose a project.

1 **Make an ad promoting clean fun.**

· Brainstorm ways to have fun that don't harm the environment.

· Plan and write a script for an ad that promotes environmentally friendly fun.

· Film your ad and show it to the class.

2 **Write a song about the environment.**

· Brainstorm some environmental topics that matter to you.

· Write your lyrics and add music.

· Perform your song!

3 **Reduce the footprint of fun at your school.**

· Choose an upcoming event at your school.

· Develop a plan to reduce litter produced at the event.

· Make posters or flyers to promote your ideas.

Express Yourself

REDUCE,

Inbox>

From: events@impactcommunityschool.edu

To: friends@impactcommunityschool.edu

Subject: **Invitation to our fundraising concert: Reduce, re-use, recycle, rock!**

It's that time of year again when we all come together for our annual fundraiser concert. Last year's event was a huge success, but this year will be even better because it will be completely green! We want to have fun and raise money, but we also want to keep our footprint small. Big changes are being made to achieve that goal. Click on the invitation to learn more. Hope to see you there!

VIEW INVITATION →

RE-USE, RECYCLE, ROCK!

WHEN: 22nd April at 3.00 P.M.

WHERE: Impact Park

COST: €15.00 in advance,
€20.00 at the event

(Remember, all of the money raised benefits Impact Community School!)

We're reducing our festival footprint by:

· using biofuel tour buses for band transport
· powering lights with solar energy
· offering only local organic food options
· providing compostable plates and utensils

You can reduce your festival footprint by:

· not printing this invitation
· bringing your own refillable water bottle
· walking, cycling or car sharing to the venue
· forwarding this invitation to a friend

2 **Discuss in groups.**

1. Does the invitation make you want to attend the festival? Why or why not?

2. Name two other ways that the festival organisers could help guests reduce their footprint of fun.

3 **Connect ideas.** In Unit 3, you learnt about sustainable eating. In Unit 4, you learnt about having fun responsibly. What connection can you see between the two units?

4 **YOU DECIDE** **Choose an activity.**

1. Choose a topic:
   • sustainable fun
   • sustainable food

2. Choose a way to express yourself:
   • an online invitation
   • a slideshow
   • a poster

3. Present your work.

75

Why We Explore

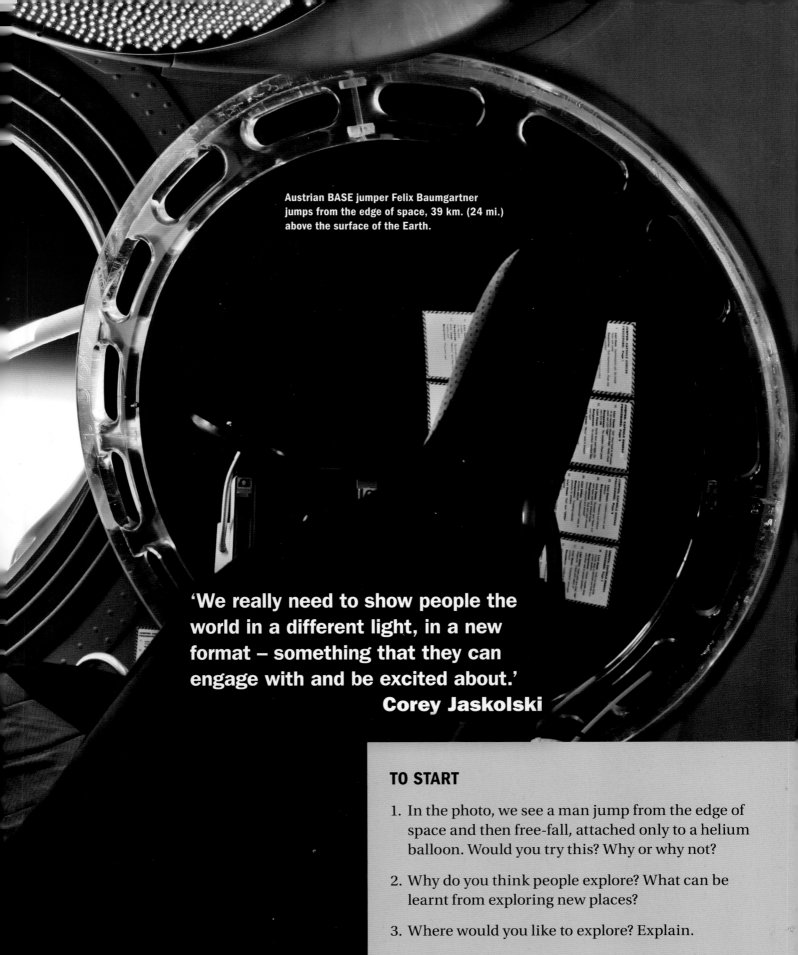

Austrian BASE jumper Felix Baumgartner jumps from the edge of space, 39 km. (24 mi.) above the surface of the Earth.

'We really need to show people the world in a different light, in a new format – something that they can engage with and be excited about.'
Corey Jaskolski

TO START

1. In the photo, we see a man jump from the edge of space and then free-fall, attached only to a helium balloon. Would you try this? Why or why not?

2. Why do you think people explore? What can be learnt from exploring new places?

3. Where would you like to explore? Explain.

1 Why do we explore? Discuss. Then listen and read. ∩ 057

The desire for **knowledge** about our world pushes explorers into the smallest caves, the deepest oceans and even outer space. People have been exploring for centuries. But any explorer will tell you that the more they **investigate**, the more they realise there's still so much to learn.

Explorer Sylvia Earle is a deep-sea **pioneer** with a long list of achievements. She has engaged in 7,000 hours of underwater study and written nearly 200 scientific articles on her findings. In 1970, she and a team of women 'aquanauts' were required to live underwater for weeks at a time to **research** marine life. The fact that so much of the ocean remains undiscovered **has driven** Sylvia's work. In fact, even though explorers have been studying the world's oceans for years, they've only seen about five per cent of them! Sylvia's **purpose** in life has been to protect the sea, and she encourages others to do so as well.

Palaeoanthropologist Lee Berger has been searching for ancient remains in **remote** parts of Africa for over two decades. He is **curious** about the origins of human beings. Lee has made some **exciting**

discoveries over time, but his most important discovery came in 2014 when he led an expedition at the Rising Star cave system, near Johannesburg, South Africa. To explore one of the caves, researchers had to squeeze through an opening less than 25 cm. (10 in.) wide. Lee wasn't small enough to do it himself, so he gathered an **expert** team of female researchers who made it inside. There they found over 1,550 bones, representing at least 15 individuals.

The bones were brought to the lab where skeletons were assembled. Lee used 3D scanning to identify an entirely new species. Creating the skeleton was just the first step in understanding the new species. 'The discoveries we're now making show that, in some ways, the age of exploration is still just beginning,' says Lee.

Engineer and inventor Corey Jaskolski not only explores, but also creates **high-tech** tools that allow people to **look into** the past without harming its artefacts. Corey wants explorers to protect what they **encounter** so that future generations can learn from them, too. 'When we discover things, we have a responsibility to preserve them as well,' he says.

Scientists working inside the Rising Star cave.

2. **LEARN NEW WORDS Listen and repeat.** 🎧 058

3. **Work in pairs.** Why do you think each explorer's contributions are important? How does an explorer's work matter to all of us?

4 **Read and write the words from the list.** Make any necessary changes.

curious	drive	encounter	exciting	expert
high-tech	investigate	knowledge	purpose	remote

Corey Jaskolski is an _____ engineer and inventor whose _____ inventions are helping explorers – and ordinary people – to see the world in a different way. For example, his underwater robotic cameras can get high-resolution photos of very _____ parts of the ocean. These devices were used to _____ and film the *Titanic* shipwreck. Corey has also developed 360-degree viewers for the _____ of allowing people to explore _____ places, such as King Tut's tomb, just by moving their mobile devices! Corey also has created night-vision cameras and 3D camera traps that help photographers capture images of animals without disturbing them. Conservation is what _____ much of Corey's work. His equipment can be used to gain _____ about places or animals without harming them at all. Corey wants to protect what's here on Earth so that future generations can enjoy exploring just like he does.

Corey Jaskolski

5 **LEARN NEW WORDS Listen to these words and match them to their definitions.** Then listen and repeat. 🎧 059 060

achievement	encourage	engage in	require

_____ 1. help or support someone

_____ 2. need something or make something necessary

_____ 3. be involved in a cause

_____ 4. success

6 **YOU DECIDE Choose an activity.**

1. **Work independently.** How well do you know your community? Investigate your area. Explore both online and 'in the field'. Share your experience with the class.

2. **Work in pairs.** How might technology help in making new discoveries? Make a list of five ideas. Present your list to the class.

3. **Work in groups.** Investigate Corey's work. Which of his inventions would you like to own? What would you do with it?

Hesitating or buying time when answering questions

Where do you see yourself in five years?	Hmm, that's tough. <u>I'd like to be studying in South America, but I might need to get a job.</u>
What made you want to learn Cantonese?	Well, it's hard to explain. I guess <u>I've just always wanted to travel to Guangzhou.</u>
Why do you think humans explore?	That's a good question. Let me think about that one for a minute.

1 **Listen.** How does the speaker buy time before responding to the question? Write the phrases you hear. 🎧062

2 **Read and complete the dialogue.**

Caleb: So, Kenji, how do you like living in Canada?

Kenji: _____ I guess I'm enjoying my experience overall, but there have been some challenges.

Caleb: What's been the biggest challenge?

Kenji: _____ . Probably speaking English all the time and trying to make friends.

Caleb: But joining the baseball team has made you really popular. We're number one in the league for the first time! How did you get so good at it?

Kenji: _____ In Japan, I'm just a normal player. We practise a lot. All year, in fact. Don't you do the same with hockey?

Caleb: Some people do, but I just play for fun. Besides, I like playing baseball in spring.

Kenji: Would you like to visit Japan someday?

Caleb: _____ it'd be fun, but it sounds like I'd better get serious about baseball first!

3 **Work in pairs.** Cut out the cards on page 165. Take turns asking each other the questions on the cards. Use the phrases above to buy time when necessary.

> Hmm, that's a good question. I'd really like to go to Borneo.

> If you could go anywhere in the world, where would you go?

4 **Work in groups.** Write five original questions to ask your group. Then take turns asking and answering your questions.

> What is your favourite book?

> Hmm, that's a tough one. Let me think about that.

Go to page 165.

Narrative tenses: Telling a story

Barrington Irving **had been preparing** to become a pilot since he was 15.

He **found** a manufacturer to build an aeroplane from donated parts that he **had received**.

On the day of the flight, he **was** ready, but he **was feeling** a little nervous.

Finally, Barrington **set off** on his historic flight. He **flew** around the world in 97 days and set a world record.

1 **Listen.** Answer the questions below using the narrative tenses. ∩ 064

1. What career had Barrington been preparing for?
   _____

2. What happened when Barrington met a Jamaican pilot?
   _____

3. How did he start learning to fly?
   _____

4. What had he been offered? Did he accept the offer?
   _____

5. What was Barrington doing before his first solo flight?
   _____

6. How was his first solo flight?
   _____

2 **Read.** Underline the narrative tenses in the paragraph.

3 **Write.** Re-read the prompt from Activity 2. Write your own response using the narrative tenses. Then share your response in a group.

Prompt: Talk about a time when you achieved something important. What did you achieve? How had you been preparing?

Once I climbed a mountain that was over 3,000 m. (10,000 ft.) tall. I had been training with my dad all spring to get ready. We had been practising on smaller mountains. To climb the mountain, we were using special equipment like ice picks and thick ropes. After we had reached the top, it felt great to look down on the forest below us. I later climbed three other mountains with my dad, and we plan to do another next month.

4 **LEARN NEW WORDS** Listen to the story of
Barrington's first solo flight around the world.
Then listen and repeat. 🎧 065 066

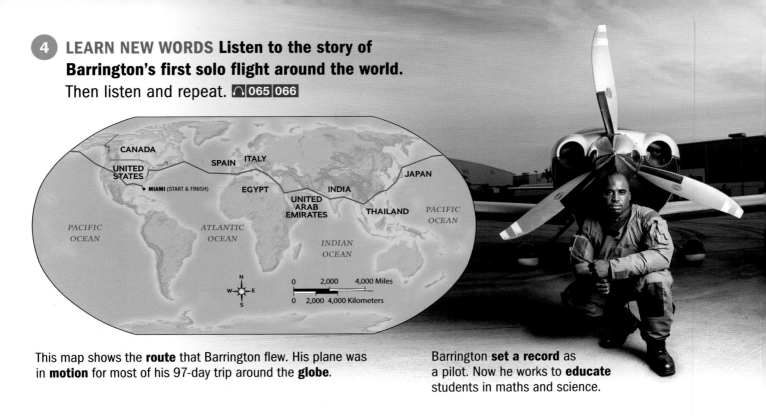

This map shows the **route** that Barrington flew. His plane was
in **motion** for most of his 97-day trip around the **globe**.

Barrington **set a record** as
a pilot. Now he works to **educate**
students in maths and science.

5 **Work in pairs.** Read the interview questions and fill in the blanks with the correct words from
the box. Then answer the questions as if you were Barrington. Use the narrative tenses.

globe	motion	pilot	route	set a record

1. Q: How had playing video games prepared you to become a _____ ?

   A: _____

2. Q: How were you able to get an aeroplane to fly around the _____ ?

   A: _____

3. Q: How many stops were on your _____ ?

   A: _____

4. Q: What were you doing to stay awake while in _____ for so
   many hours?

   A: _____

5. Q: How did you feel when you heard you had _____ ?

   A: _____

6 **Work independently.** Investigate another person who has explored new places.
Write a narrative about the explorer's route, experiences and accomplishments.
Share what you learnt with the class.

THE Explorer GENE

Are we born to explore?

Of all the animals on Earth, none are so driven to explore as humans. Other animals will go in search of food or water. But humans can be motivated simply by the possibility of discovery. So what is it exactly that caused us to spread out across the globe 60,000 years ago, instead of just staying in Africa?

Perhaps it's in our DNA. In 1999, Dr Chuansheng Chen led a team of scientists who were studying a gene known as $DRD_{4-7}R$. This gene is found in about 20 per cent of all humans. It's been associated with higher rates of risk-taking, exploration and interest in new ideas. Dr Chen found that $DRD_{4-7}R$ is more common in societies that move around a lot than those who don't. For example, studies in Africa show that the gene is much more common in nomadic tribes than in tribes that prefer to stay in one place. Several other researchers have studied this topic and found additional evidence to support Dr Chen's claim.

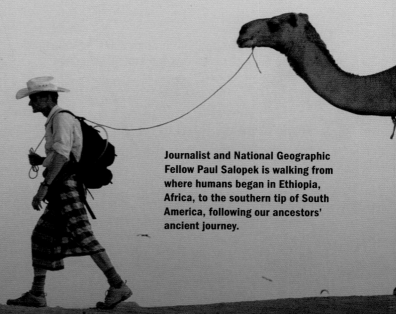

Journalist and National Geographic Fellow Paul Salopek is walking from where humans began in Ethiopia, Africa, to the southern tip of South America, following our ancestors' ancient journey.

1 BEFORE YOU READ **Discuss in pairs.** Based on the title and the photo, what do you think you'll learn in this reading?

2 LEARN NEW WORDS **Find these words in the reading.** What do you think they mean? Look at how they're pronounced in a dictionary. Say them aloud. Then listen and repeat. ∩ 067

| associated | gene | motivate | trait |

3 WHILE YOU READ **Think about a person you know who might have the explorer gene.** ∩ 068

But can a single gene be responsible for a trait as complex as the desire to explore? Dr Kenneth Kidd doesn't think so. He thinks $DRD_{4-7}R$ might increase curiosity, but other equally important sets of genes give us intelligent minds and skilled hands. We then use our minds and hands to create things. He believes that not just one gene, but groups of genes work together to create complex behaviours like exploration.

The context we live in also plays a role in our desire to explore. For example, during the European Age of Exploration, explorers became rich and famous for their discoveries. This drove others to try to increase their wealth through exploration. In this case, their exploration was more likely motivated by money than by genes.

Maybe the desire to explore comes from something inside us, such as the $DRD_{4-7}R$ gene. Or maybe it has more to do with what's happening in the world around us. Maybe both. Whatever the reason, it seems we (or at least some of us) will keep exploring the mountains, the sea, the stars and beyond, because that's just what humans do.

4 AFTER YOU READ **Work in pairs to answer the questions.**

1. What makes humans explore? How are we different from other animals?
2. What traits is the $DRD_{4-7}R$ gene associated with?
3. What percentage of humans have this gene?
4. What is Dr Kenneth Kidd's opinion regarding $DRD_{4-7}R$'s connection to exploration?
5. What else might cause humans to explore?

5 **Work in pairs.** Describe the person that you thought of in Activity 3. Give examples to explain why you think this person has the gene.

6 **Discuss in groups.**

1. Do you believe a gene causes humans to explore? Or do you think it has more to do with other factors? Explain.
2. Do you think you have the $DRD_{4-7}R$ gene? Explain, with examples. What other beliefs and behaviours might be caused by something in your genes?
3. Are humans exploring more now than in the past? Will we ever stop exploring? Explain.

1 **BEFORE YOU WATCH Discuss in pairs.** Why is it important to explore?

2 **WHILE YOU WATCH Complete the quotes.** Watch scene 5.1.

1. 'It's part of _____ to be _____ and to want to learn more about the world.'

2. 'It _____ . I mean that's what exploring is about.'

3. 'We think we know _____ , but we don't. We think we know _____ , but we don't. We think we _____ , but we don't.'

4. 'By knowing what's out there, we _____ .'

Explorers camping near the Nyiragongo volcano, Democratic Republic of the Congo

3 **Read and circle the correct letter.**

1. Which of the following reasons for exploring is not mentioned in the video?
   a. Exploring helps us engage more fully with our world.
   b. Exploring will make us famous.
   c. Exploring is part of human nature.

2. Why is it important to care about what's out there?
   a. So that we can stop asking questions
   b. So that we can engage with our world and act with love
   c. Because very few people do

3. What do we use to help us explore?
   a. Information about the people who came before us
   b. Information about new species of animals
   c. The high-tech tools of science

4. Why is technology important for exploration?
   a. Because without technology, it's impossible to discover any new animal species.
   b. Because it lets us explore places that are otherwise inaccessible.
   c. Because technology is so important for conservation.

4 **Work in pairs.** Review your answer for Activity 1. Compare it with what you heard in the video. Discuss your comparisons with your partner.

5 **Work in groups.** You're in charge of a school-wide campaign to promote exploration. Create a poster or an advertisement on the benefits of exploring. Present your work to the class.

6 **YOU DECIDE** **Choose an activity.**

1. **Work independently.** Research one of the explorers from the video to learn more about his/her work. Share what you learnt with the class.

2. **Work in pairs.** Make your own video, similar to this one. Interview other students and ask them, 'What can we learn from exploring our region?'

3. **Work in groups.** Research a recent discovery of a new species. Find out who the explorers were, where they went and what led them to the discovery.

Geographic use of *the*

I'm going to **the Himalayas** to climb **Mount Everest**.

The Yangtze is the longest river in **Asia**. **Lake Baikal** is the largest lake in **Asia**.

The equator passes through **Isabella Island**, the largest of **the Galápagos Islands**.

Explorer Ferdinand Magellan was born in **Portugal**, but died in **the Philippines**.

Explorer Gertrude Bell wrote a book about **Syria** after her travels to **the Middle East**.

1 **Read.** Fill in the timeline of female explorers by adding *the* when necessary.

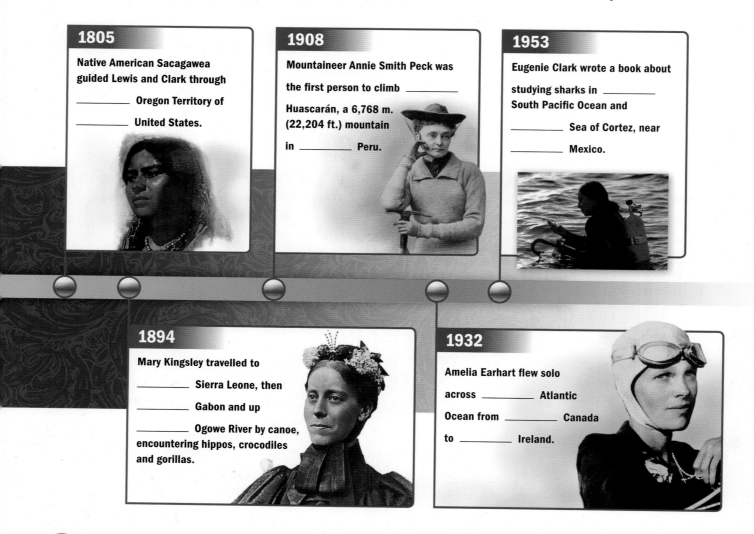

1805

Native American Sacagawea guided Lewis and Clark through _____ Oregon Territory of _____ United States.

1908

Mountaineer Annie Smith Peck was the first person to climb _____ Huascarán, a 6,768 m. (22,204 ft.) mountain in _____ Peru.

1953

Eugenie Clark wrote a book about studying sharks in _____ South Pacific Ocean and _____ Sea of Cortez, near _____ Mexico.

1894

Mary Kingsley travelled to _____ Sierra Leone, then _____ Gabon and up _____ Ogowe River by canoe, encountering hippos, crocodiles and gorillas.

1932

Amelia Earhart flew solo across _____ Atlantic Ocean from _____ Canada to _____ Ireland.

2 **Work in pairs.** Cut out the cards and place them face down. Take turns trying to match the information with the explorer. When you make a match, describe the explorer's work, using the places on the card.

fly solo
Jamaica
Miami
United States

Barrington Irving

Go to page 167.

WRITING

When we compare and contrast two people, things or ideas, we use phrases such as the following:

Compare: in the same way   likewise   similarly
Contrast: by comparison   in contrast   on one hand ... on the other hand

1 **Read the model.** Work in pairs to identify the parts of the writing. How does the writer compare and contrast exploration past and present? Underline the phrases.

Exploration has changed a lot over time. In the past, only adventurers who were willing to take risks were considered explorers. In contrast, anyone can be an explorer today thanks to modern technology.

In the past, when explorers travelled the world, people back home had to wait for months to hear about their adventures. Explorers kept journals and wrote letters about their experiences. They would only be able to tell others what they saw after they returned. By the end of the 19th century, explorers were also able to take photos in the same way that they do today. However, they were unable to see the photos straight away. It often took a long time for them to get photos printed.

By comparison, today's explorers can travel around the globe and can send back live, real-time images. Thanks to high-tech devices and the Internet, anyone can interact with them. When a discovery is made, we can see photos on social media and read blog posts the same day. We may not be there, but we still take part in the adventure. Similarly, thanks to high-tech cameras and 3D scanners, archaeologists and other scientists can now study objects without ever touching or removing them from their sites. This way, people can learn about these things without the risk of harming or breaking them.

There are similarities between exploration in the past and the present. For example, explorers are driven by curiosity and the desire for knowledge about the world. Likewise, people want to share what they discover with others, both in writing and with photos. So, even though the methods may be different, our reasons for exploring have stayed the same over time.

2 **Work in pairs.** How is the way we explore different now compared to the past?

3 **Write.** Write an essay that compares and contrasts exploring out in the field with exploring virtually.

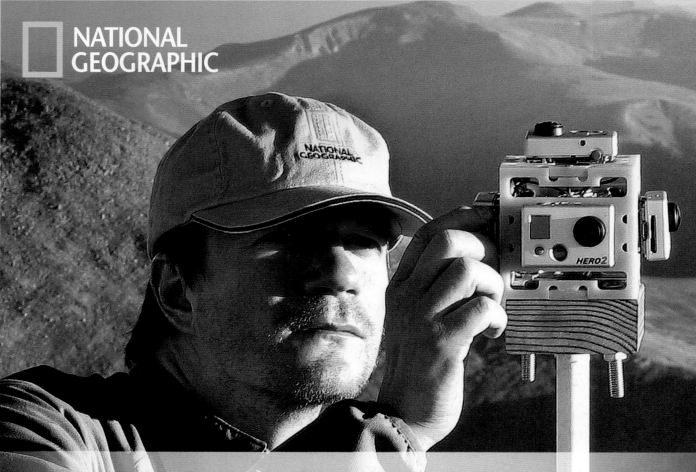

NATIONAL GEOGRAPHIC

Learn by Doing

'If you have curiosity, you have to be an explorer. You have to go out and find the answers yourself without waiting to get them from others.'

Corey Jaskolski
National Geographic Explorer, Engineer/Inventor

1. **Watch scene 5.2.**

2. How do you learn best – by listening to your teacher or by doing something for yourself? What are the advantages of each type of learning? Talk about a time when you learnt something new just by doing it.

3. When you go to a new place, what tools do you use to help you explore? What other tools could you use to learn about another place? Name two or three that you would like to have.

Make an Impact

YOU DECIDE Choose a project.

① Plan an expedition.

· Research where you will explore and what you hope to find.

· Plan your expedition. Create an itinerary with photos and a map showing where you plan to explore. Add as much detail as possible.

· Present your plan to the class.

② Profile a well-known explorer.

· Research an explorer from the past or present.

· Prepare a biography of the explorer. Include information on where he/she has explored, what he/she has discovered, and his/her methods and tools.

· Create a poster or a computer-based presentation to share what you learnt.

③ Explore from home.

· Research different ways to explore without leaving your home.

· Identify advantages and disadvantages of virtual exploration.

· Write a feature article to describe ways for people to explore virtually. Use examples from your own experience.

Giants

'For as long as humans have been around, they have been fascinated by giant organisms.'

Nizar Ibrahim

TO START

1. Look at the tree. How old do you think it is? What makes you think this?

2. What's the biggest plant you've ever seen in real life? The biggest animal? Describe them.

3. What do you think of when you hear the word *giant*? Why?

A team of scientists measuring a giant sequoia in Sequoia National Park, California, USA

Who were the giants of the past?
Discuss. Then listen and read. 🎧 070

Let's go back, deep in time, to the land of the giants, when there were hundreds of species of dinosaurs on Earth. What were they like? And how did they go extinct? Many scientists believe that a major **catastrophe** – a meteor strike – destroyed these **enormous** beasts. Even though they've gone, their fossils can help us to understand what they were like.

Many people think that *Tyrannosaurus rex*, or *T. rex*, is the king of the **ancient** carnivores. It's *T. rex's* size that made this creature so **frightening** – it was **huge!** *T. rex* measured 4.5–6 m. (15–20 ft.) tall and 12 m. (40 ft.) long. Its eyes were the size of grapefruits; its **stomach** was 1 m. (3.3 ft.) in **diameter,** and it used its massive **jaws** to chew up to 230 kg. (500 lbs.) of meat in a single bite! *T. rex* had a **heart** the size of a refrigerator, which pumped all the blood through its giant body.

Although *T. rex* was really big, it wasn't the largest **prehistoric** creature ever discovered. That title belongs to *Argentinosaurus*, who measured 40 m. (130 ft.) long. This gigantic herbivore's bones were found in Patagonia, Argentina. Babies **weighed** only 5 kg. (11 lb.), but adults could weigh up to 70 tonnes. To reach full size, a young *Argentinosaurus* must have gained up to 5 kg. per day over 40 years, which made it one of the fastest-growing animals on Earth!

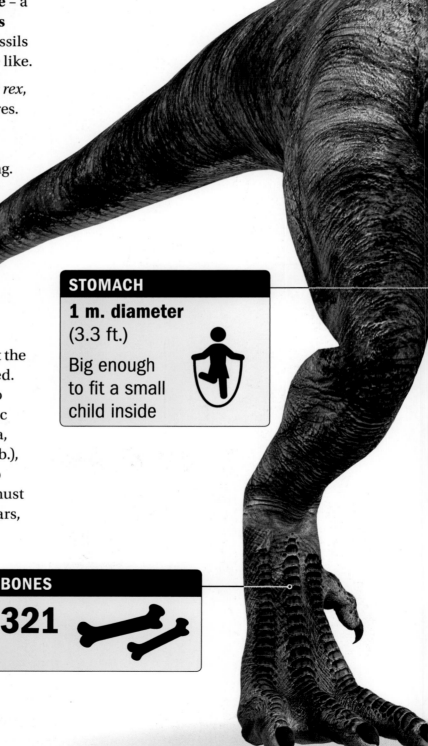

STOMACH

1 m. diameter
(3.3 ft.)

Big enough to fit a small child inside

BONES

321

BRAIN

30 cm. diameter
(11 in.)

Shaped like a
head of broccoli

TEETH

30 cm. long
(11 in.)

HEART

75 x 50 x 50 cm.
(30 x 20 x 20 in.)

The size of
a small
refrigerator

Dinosaurs lived on Earth for around
165 million years – a lot longer than humans
have. Some never completely disappeared:
they just became much smaller. Eventually,
they **developed** into the birds of today.
Palaeontologists remind us that most
species eventually face **extinction**,
and humans may be no **exception**
to that rule. But by studying how
dinosaurs lived, we might just learn
how to extend our own stay here on Earth well
into the future.

2 **LEARN NEW WORDS Listen and repeat.** 🎧 **071**

3 **Work in pairs.** Think about the largest animals
on Earth today. Research their sizes. How would
they compare to *T. rex*? To *Argentinosaurus*?

4 Read and write the words from the list. Make any necessary changes.

ancient	catastrophe	develop	extinction
frightening	huge	jaw	weigh

　　　Nizar Ibrahim has always loved dinosaurs. As a student, he _____ an interest in the work of a famous palaeontologist, Dr Ernst Stromer. One hundred years ago, Dr Stromer collected bones from the _____ sands of the Sahara Desert. About 100 million years ago, the Sahara Desert was a tropical waterway full of _____ predatory giants. Today, Nizar is continuing to learn about what lived in this region. He's most interested in Dr Stromer's discovery of *Spinosaurus*, a skilled hunter that could catch food in water and on land. *Spinosaurus* was _____ – even bigger than *T. rex*. In fact, *Spinosaurus* had metre-long _____ that it used for catching fish and other aquatic creatures. Dr Stromer was the first to make significant discoveries about *Spinosaurus*, but Nizar has found more remains of this fascinating giant than anyone else to date.

5 LEARN NEW WORDS Listen for these words. Write *S* next to word pairs that are synonyms and *A* next to antonyms. Then listen and repeat. 🎧 072 073

Nizar Ibrahim

carnivore	gigantic	herbivore	massive

_____ 1. carnivore　　herbivore

_____ 2. massive　　small

_____ 3. enormous　　massive

_____ 4. tiny　　gigantic

_____ 5. gigantic　　huge

_____ 6. herbivore　　plant-eater

6 YOU DECIDE Choose an activity.

1. **Work independently.** Make a poster about a dinosaur you hadn't heard of before. Describe its size, diet, habitat, when it lived and other characteristics.

2. **Work in pairs.** Research the dinosaurs that once lived in your region. Compare them with wild animals that live in this region today.

3. **Work in groups.** Talk about an encounter with a large animal you've had at a zoo or in the wild.

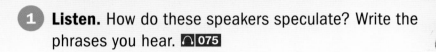

Speculating about the past and the future

In theory, <u>dinosaurs were destroyed by a global catastrophe</u>.

What may have happened <u>is that they evolved into smaller animals, such as birds</u>.

I wonder <u>how humans will evolve over the next thousand years</u>.

Is it possible that <u>we will become totally different creatures</u>?

It could be that <u>we'll be exactly the same in the year 3000</u>.

1 **Listen.** How do these speakers speculate? Write the phrases you hear. 075

2 **Read and complete the dialogue.**

Nina: _____ which
dinosaurs had hair on their bodies.

Rene: You mean fur, like bears and lions have?

Nina: Yes. You know, we only know what their bones were like, so
_____ , some could have had fur or feathers.

Scientists believe that the large, feathered *Yutyrannus* was 9 m. (30 ft.) long and weighed about 1,400 kg. (3,000 lb.).

Rene: _____ *T. rex* was soft and furry?

Nina: Actually, they found a dinosaur similar to *T. rex* in China that was covered in soft feathers – like a baby chick!

Rene: Wow! A massive baby chick? Sounds like a horror film!

Nina: Well, the ones they found were smaller than *T. rex*, but still about the length of a city bus.

Rene: That's pretty big. _____ why they had feathers?

Nina: _____ is that some dinosaurs grew feathers and fur to stay warm in colder climates.

3 **Work in groups.** Cut four strips of paper. Write a question about a prehistoric giant on each of the strips. Mix the group's questions into a single pile. Take turns asking questions and speculating.

I wonder what *T. rex*'s skin was like.

It could be that *T. rex* had very colourful skin.

4 **Work in groups.** Repeat the activity above. This time, choose your own topics to discuss.

Is it possible that our school will offer a class in palaeontology?

GRAMMAR 🎧 076

Relative clauses: Defining and describing

I learnt about megalodon in a documentary **that/which** was very informative. It had enormous teeth **that/which** were as sharp as knives.

Scientists **who/that** study sharks believe that megalodon is a distant cousin of the modern great white shark.

The ocean **where/in which** megalodon swam was much warmer than the ocean is today.

Megalodon, **which** was a fierce predator, was able to catch the largest whales.

Scientists such as Catalina Pimiento, **who** researches sharks, have studied reasons for megalodon's extinction.

Megalodon, **whose** name comes from the Greek *giant tooth*, had enormous jaws.

1 Read. Complete the sentences below with *that*, *which*, *where*, *who* or *whose*.

Many people today fear the great white shark, _____ is considered the fiercest predator of the seas. The great white's enormous size is enough to scare off anybody _____ comes near it. This carnivore, _____ measures 4.5–6 m. (15–20 ft.), is often believed to prey on humans. In fact, researchers, _____ job it is to study shark attacks, have determined that the species is responsible for between one-third and one-half of all shark attacks. But the idea _____ the great white seeks out humans who swim in the waters _____ it lives isn't based in reality. Although we're talking about a shark _____ is known for biting, the great white is really just a curious animal. When it sees a human _____ crosses its path, the shark will most likely bite and then release the victim. The fact _____ the great white could bite just because it's curious isn't very comforting. The only good news is that the great white shark, while enormous, is much closer in size to us than its distant cousin, megalodon, a creature _____ was more than double (maybe triple!) its size.

2 Work in pairs. Look at Activity 1 again. Cross out any relative clauses that can be removed from the paragraph.

3 **LEARN NEW WORDS Listen to the information about megalodon.** Then listen and repeat. 🎧 **077** **078**

Megalodon
Ancient Giant of the Sea

Lived 16 million years ago – 2 million years ago, during the Miocene **era**

Teeth as long as 18 cm. (7 in.) – about 50 **times** the size of a human tooth

Fierce predator that **preyed on** whales and other giant sea creatures

4 **Read and write.** Combine the sentences into one. Use *that, which, where, who* and *whose*.

1. Megalodon was a fierce predator. It was almost three times the size of *T. rex.*
   Megalodon, which was a fierce predator, was almost three times the size of T. rex.

2. Megalodon was known for its massive teeth. Its teeth were 18 cm. (7 in.) long.
   _____

3. Megalodon had three rows of teeth. Its teeth were as sharp as knives.
   _____

4. Megalodon and whales swam in oceans around the world. Researchers find their remains together in the oceans.
   _____

5. Megalodon lived during the Miocene era. The Miocene era began about 23 million years ago.
   _____

6. Some scientists look for reasons why megalodon went extinct. Their job is to study megalodon.
   _____

5 **Work in groups.** Choose your own topic and write three clues about it on a piece of paper. Use *that, which, where, who* and *whose* in your sentences. Then read your clue aloud to your group members, who will guess what you're talking about.

This is the teacher whose job is to teach us about how animals evolve.

It's our biology teacher, Mr Johnson.

1 BEFORE YOU READ Discuss in pairs. You've been learning about dinosaurs in this unit. Look at the image below. What's different about the dinosaur you'll read about?

2 LEARN NEW WORDS Find these words in the reading. What do you think they mean? Notice the word parts and think about what each part means. Then listen and repeat. 🎧079

advantage	extraordinary
significant	useless

3 WHILE YOU READ Think about how Nizar must have felt about finding *Spinosaurus* remains. 🎧080

Nizar Ibrahim has always been fascinated by dinosaurs. And he's always enjoyed travelling to faraway places. As a palaeontologist, he's able to do both. Nizar has spent a lot of time in the Kem Kem, a region in the Sahara Desert along the border of Morocco and Algeria. This region is hot and dry now, but it was once home to a large river where amazing creatures lived: car-sized fish, several different types of crocodile-like creatures and a large, predatory dinosaur called *Spinosaurus*.

Spinosaurus, which lived in North Africa about 97 million years ago, was an extraordinary creature. It was enormous, with a length of up to 15 m. (50 ft.). It had massive jaws like a crocodile, which were an advantage when catching prey. Nizar knew about some of these characteristics from research that had been done on the *Spinosaurus* in the early 1900s by German palaeontologist Ernst Stromer. Nizar and his colleagues used Professor Stromer's notes and sketches, the fossils he had found and CT-scanning technology to piece together a whole *Spinosaurus* skeleton – a digital dinosaur.

What Nizar and his team learnt was significant: *Spinosaurus* had dense bones, feet like paddles and small hind limbs. All of these were characteristic of animals that spent a lot of

Spinosaurus

DISCOVERING
Spinosaurus

How one determined palaeontologist found a river monster in the Sahara time in the water. 'We realised that we were dealing with a river monster,' said Nizar. 'A predatory dinosaur bigger than *T. rex*, the ruler of this ancient river of giants.'

Perhaps the only thing more amazing than the creature itself is how Nizar was able to find its skeleton. In 2008, a local man from Erfoud, Morocco, gave Nizar a cardboard box filled with some fossils. A little while later, Italian colleagues contacted Nizar about fossils they received that were extremely similar to the ones he was given. Nizar wanted to find where the fossils came from. If only Nizar could find the man from Erfoud! Nizar didn't even know the man's name. He only had a mental image of a man with a moustache, which wasn't very helpful. Nizar travelled to Morocco anyway, to try to find him. After a long, unsuccessful search, Nizar gave up hope. He was sitting at an outdoor café, drinking tea with a colleague, talking about how it was useless: he would never piece together *Spinosaurus*. Suddenly, he looked up and saw the man walking down the street. He had found the missing link! The fossil hunter took Nizar to the site, and he was finally able to locate the remaining bones for his *Spinosaurus* skeleton.

4 **AFTER YOU READ Work in pairs to decide if each sentence is *true* or *false*.** Tick the correct answer.

1. The Kem Kem region has a large river running through it. Ⓣ Ⓕ

2. Nizar was the first scientist to discover *Spinosaurus*. Ⓣ Ⓕ

3. *Spinosaurus* was larger than *T. rex*. Ⓣ Ⓕ

4. The only thing that really helped Nizar understand *Spinosaurus* was the CT-scanning technology. Ⓣ Ⓕ

5. Dense bones, feet like paddles and small hind limbs are characteristics of animals that spend time in the water. Ⓣ Ⓕ

6. The man in Morocco gave Nizar all of *Spinosaurus's* bones in a cardboard box. Ⓣ Ⓕ

5 **Work independently.** Imagine you're Nizar. Write a journal entry about finding the *Spinosaurus* bones. How does the discovery make you feel? Why?

6 **Discuss in groups.**

1. What are the advantages of studying dinosaurs? What are the challenges facing palaeontologists? Is it worth it to study dinosaurs? Why or why not?

2. What personality traits does Nizar have that helped him to find *Spinosaurus*? Do you have any of these traits? How do you use them?

3. Nizar uses new technology, combined with fossils and old documents, to understand *Spinosaurus*. Name another way that new technology can be used to help people understand something very old.

Nizar and his team looking for fossils in the Sahara

1 BEFORE YOU WATCH **Discuss in pairs.**

1. Look again at the photo on pages 92–93. Comment on the size of the tree in comparison with the people.

2. Look at the timeline on this page. Note the dates when it begins and ends. What do you think they represent?

2 **Work in pairs.** The title of this video is *Super Tree*. You'll see a team of photographers and scientists photographing one of the largest trees in the world, in winter. Predict three challenges that they face.

3 WHILE YOU WATCH **Check your predictions from Activity 2.** Were they correct? Did the team face any other challenges? What were they? **Watch scene 6.1.**

4 AFTER YOU WATCH **Work in pairs.** Answer the questions below.

1. What makes the President unique?

2. Describe the President in relation to yourself.

3. How long did it take the team to prepare for the photo shoot? Why do you think that is?

4. Why did these scientists go through so much effort to photograph a tree?

5. The team thinks that the President may be the biggest tree because it has the most biomass. What do you think the word *biomass* means?

2012
Scientists climb the President, the second-largest living tree.

1969
The first person lands on the moon.

1707
Mount Fuji erupts in Japan.

1325
The Aztecs establish the city of Tenochtitlan.

868 CE
The earliest known book is printed.

221 BCE
Construction of the Great Wall of China begins.

1100 BCE
Nearly 100 years after this tree sprouts, people begin making iron tools.

---

5 **Work in pairs.** Read and cross out the false sentences. Then rewrite them correctly.

1. There is only one species of California redwoods.

   _____

2. The bigger the tree, the less it's producing.

   _____

3. The President has been growing for over 3,000 years.

   _____

4. At over 8 m. (27 ft.) in diameter, the President has the largest trunk of any tree.

   _____

   _____

5. The horrible snowstorm is making the team members want to cry.

   _____

   _____

6 **Work in groups.** Look at the timeline. Think of five more significant events that have happened during this tree's lifetime. List them in the order they occur.

7 **YOU DECIDE** **Choose an activity.**

1. **Work independently.** Photograph something very large in your community. Make sure you get the entire object into your photograph. Display your photo(s) in class and talk about the process of capturing the object.

2. **Work in pairs.** In the video, scientists work together to photograph a big tree. Think of another situation you've heard or read about where people came together to work with a big animal or plant. Why are so many people needed to work with giant things?

3. **Work in groups.** Find out about another well-known big tree. Say where it is, how big it is and how old it is. Share a photo and describe it.

VIDEO **103**

GRAMMAR ∩081

Reduction of relative clauses

My brother, **(who is) a filmmaker**, created a documentary about manta rays.

The documentaries **(that) I was telling you about** deal with sea creatures.

One of the documentaries is about a new species **(that/which was) discovered** last year.

The scientists **(that/who) I saw** in the documentaries were really interesting.

The biologist **that/who studies** manta rays lives in Mozambique. (The biologist **studying** manta rays …)

1 **Read.** Cross out unnecessary words to reduce the clauses.

You read about the giants of the past. But there are plenty of giants still alive today who are living in the sea. The blue whale, which is the largest animal of all time, is still with us today. Many other giants live underwater as well. Andrea Marshall, who is a conservation biologist, studies these *marine megafauna*, or giant, underwater animals. Much of her work focuses on the enormous manta rays that are living off the coast of Mozambique. Manta rays are

threatened because they're being harmed by human activity and they don't reproduce often. In 2009, Andrea founded the Marine Megafauna Foundation, which is an organisation that works to protect large marine animals such as the manta ray. One of her proudest moments came in 2013, which was the year she got special protection for the manta ray. 'Mantas are some of the most engaging and charismatic underwater animals you'll ever encounter,' says Andrea. 'They're so curious and clever, always ready to interact and play with you.'

A manta ray

2 **Read.** Rewrite the sentences, reducing the clauses.

1. Biologist Andrea Marshall, who is known for protecting marine megafauna, focuses on the manta ray.
   Biologist Andrea Marshall, known for protecting marine megafauna, focuses on the manta ray.
2. The manta rays that Marshall studies don't reproduce very often.

   _____

3. The manta rays that swim in the waters off Mozambique are in need of protection.

   _____

3 **Work in groups.** Cut out the cards. Take turns reading the sentences aloud and reducing the clauses.

Go to page 169.

The T. rex, which was the fiercest land predator of its time, had huge jaws and teeth.

WRITING

When writing a news report, we should consider the five *W*s: *who*, *what*, *where*, *when* and *why*, as well as *how*. Answering these questions early on can capture the reader's interest and make him/her want to learn more. Answering these questions will also provide all the necessary details about the situation in the report.

1 **Read the model.** Work in pairs. Identify the five *W*s and *how* in the news report.

Capturing a Giant: Enormous Tree Photographed in Sequoia National Park

Sequoia National Park, California, is the land of the giants. The giants are the sequoias, the largest species of trees on the planet. A few among them are so extraordinary they have names. The President is one of the largest trees in the world. It was recently studied by scientist Steve Sillett. In 2012, Sillett and his team photographed the entire 75 m. (246 ft.) tree. Because the tree was too large to get in one photo, Sillett's team of photographers combined several photos of the tree into one complete shot. This project was done to educate people about these enormous trees and all of the life they support.

One of the most interesting discoveries Sillett's team made is that sequoias never stop growing. As the tree continues to grow, it competes with other plants for soil, light and water. The President has been growing for 3,200 years. Because of their size, sequoias can defend themselves well against threats like wind and fire. Even lightning strikes usually fail to harm them.

The National Park Service estimates that over 260 forest plants, animals and insects depend on the sequoias, and over 150 of those life forms are rare or uncommon. Humans also depend on the sequoias to break down huge amounts of carbon dioxide, providing cleaner air for breathing.

Sillett hopes his work will not only inspire the public to help protect these giants, but also encourage more tall-tree research throughout the world.

2 **Work in pairs.** Look at the structure of the report. Where does the author answer the five *W*s? How? Does the report make you want to learn more about the topic? Why or why not?

3 **Write.** Write a news report about a giant discovery of the past or present. Use a topic from this unit or another giant discovery that interests you.

Make Big Plans

'The world is not made for us, and we are privileged to be here and should make the most of it.'

Nizar Ibrahim
National Geographic Explorer, Palaeontologist

1. **Watch scene 6.2.**

2. Nizar Ibrahim has made big plans during his career as a palaeontologist. He has already accomplished some of them. What are your big plans? When will you accomplish them?

3. Why do you think Nizar says that we're privileged to be here? Do you feel this way? Why or why not?

Make an Impact

YOU DECIDE Choose a project.

1 **Make an animated action film.**

· Write a script for an action film starring one of the giants in this unit. Draw the main scenes on separate pieces of paper.

· Place the scenes in front of a video camera. Press record and narrate the scene. Then pause, place the next scene in front of the camera and repeat.

· After all the scenes have been shot, share your film with the class.

2 **Create and play a 'Find the Fossil' game.**

· Find six different images of fossils of the giants you learnt about in this unit. Find six images of the creature to which each fossil corresponds.

· Create a memory game. Paste the fossil images on one set of cards. Paste the creatures on another set of cards.

· Place the cards face down. In pairs, take turns looking for matches. When you find a match, name the creature and one of its features. The person with the most cards wins.

3 **Plan and give a presentation on a modern giant.**

· Research the largest animals on the planet today. Choose one and learn about its size, appearance, habitat and diet.

· Create a poster or computer presentation on your animal. Include photos and statistics to illustrate its size. Compare the animal with the prehistoric giants studied in this unit.

· Make your presentation in class. Answer your classmates' questions.

Express Yourself

1 **Read and listen to the adaptation of an excerpt from *A Journey to the Centre of the Earth*.** 082

Tuesday, 18th August

Evening came, or rather the time came when sleep weighs down the tired eyes, for there is no night here. Hans was controlling the raft. During his watch, I slept.

Two hours later a terrible shock awoke me. The raft was lifted up on a very high wave, and then dropped again.

'What is the matter? Axel? Hans?' shouted my uncle, Professor Otto Lidenbrock. 'Have we struck land?'

Hans pointed with his finger at a dark mass over five hundred metres away, rising and falling in the water. I looked and cried, 'It is an enormous porpoise.'

'Yes,' replied my uncle, 'and there is a sea lizard of massive size.'

'And further on a monstrous crocodile. Look at its giant jaws and its rows of teeth! It is diving down!'

'There's a whale, a whale!' cried the professor.

We stood amazed, at the presence of such a herd of marine monsters. They were of enormous size; the smallest of them would have crunched our raft, crew and all, at one snap of its huge jaws.

Getting away was out of the question now. The reptiles rose; they circled around our little raft faster than express trains.

We stood dumb with fear. At nearly three hundred metres from us the battle was fought. We could see the two monsters engaged in deadly conflict. But it now seems to me as if the other animals were taking part, too – the porpoise, the whale, the lizard, the tortoise. Every moment I seem to see one or the other of them. I point them to Hans. He shakes his head negatively.

'*Tva*,' he says.

'What *two*? Does he mean that there are only two animals?'

'He is right,' said my uncle.

'Surely you must be mistaken,' I cried.

'No: the first of those monsters has a porpoise's snout, a lizard's head, a crocodile's teeth. It is the *ichthyosaurus* (the fish lizard), the most terrible of the ancient monsters of the deep.'

'And the other?'

'The other is a *plesiosaurus* (almost lizard), a serpent, with the characteristics of a turtle. He is the enemy of the other.'

Hans had spoken truly. Two monsters only were creating all this commotion, and before my eyes are two reptiles of the ancient world. I can distinguish the eye of the *ichthyosaurus* glowing like a red-hot coal, and as large as a man's head. This one is not less than thirty metres long, and I can judge its size when it shows its tail. Its jaw is enormous, and according to naturalists it is armed with no less than one hundred and eighty-two teeth.

The *plesiosaurus*, a serpent with a tube-shaped body and a short tail, has four flappers or paddles. Its body is entirely covered with scales, and its neck, as flexible as a swan's, rises nine metres above the waves.

Those huge creatures attacked each other with the greatest hatred.

2 **Discuss in groups.**

1. The characters are exploring the centre of the Earth. How do you imagine the centre of the Earth looks? How do the picture and the text compare with your own ideas?

2. Imagine you're on this journey. Describe how you feel when you see the ancient creatures fighting in the sea.

3. Describe the *ichthyosaurus* and the *plesiosaurus* in your own words. Compare them with the giant creatures you studied in Unit 6.

3 **Connect ideas.** In Unit 5, you learnt about exploration and discovery. In Unit 6, you learnt about giants past and present. How does the reading passage connect these two units? Do you think that real-life explorers ever had experiences similar to those of Axel, Hans and Professor Lidenbrock? Explain.

4 **YOU DECIDE** **Choose an activity.**

1. Choose a topic:
   - exploration
   - giant discoveries

2. Choose a way to express yourself:
   - the next scene of the story
   - an action/adventure skit
   - a podcast describing an adventure or a discovery

3. Present your work.

Creative Problem-Solving

A creative way to bring the
dog along, Taipei

'People create amazing things based on what they can imagine, and what they're truly, truly passionate and excited about.'

Tan Le

TO START

1. What problem is the man in the photo solving? Can you think of another way to solve the problem?

2. Think of an invention that impressed you. Who made it? How is it useful? Why is it interesting to you?

3. How does an idea become a reality? What needs to happen in order to successfully create something?

1 **What would you like to make?**
Discuss. Then listen and read. 🎧083

Have you ever had a problem you couldn't **solve**? Maybe you went to a shop to look for a solution, but came home empty-handed. More and more, when this situation occurs, people are creating their own **devices** as the solution. It's all part of the Maker Movement, made up of thousands of **resourceful** people who make and fix things, rather than buy them in shops. Makers do all sorts of **hands-on** projects, from building pizza ovens to designing their own drones. For makers, the **do-it-yourself** approach is often more affordable, sustainable and satisfying than simply looking to buy the solution to a problem.

Thanks to technology, it's easier than ever to turn a **concept** into reality. Many makers use the same tools, just in different ways. For example, Arduino® is popular among makers. This **open-source** mini controller is used to develop a variety of electronic devices. Arduino allows people to do anything from creating a talking clock to studying DNA, with very easy-to-use **hardware** and **software**. Raspberry Pi® is another popular maker tool. This mini computer is only the size of a credit card, but it's as powerful as some full-sized computers. People are using Raspberry Pi for a wide variety of **applications**, from creating video games to powering robots.

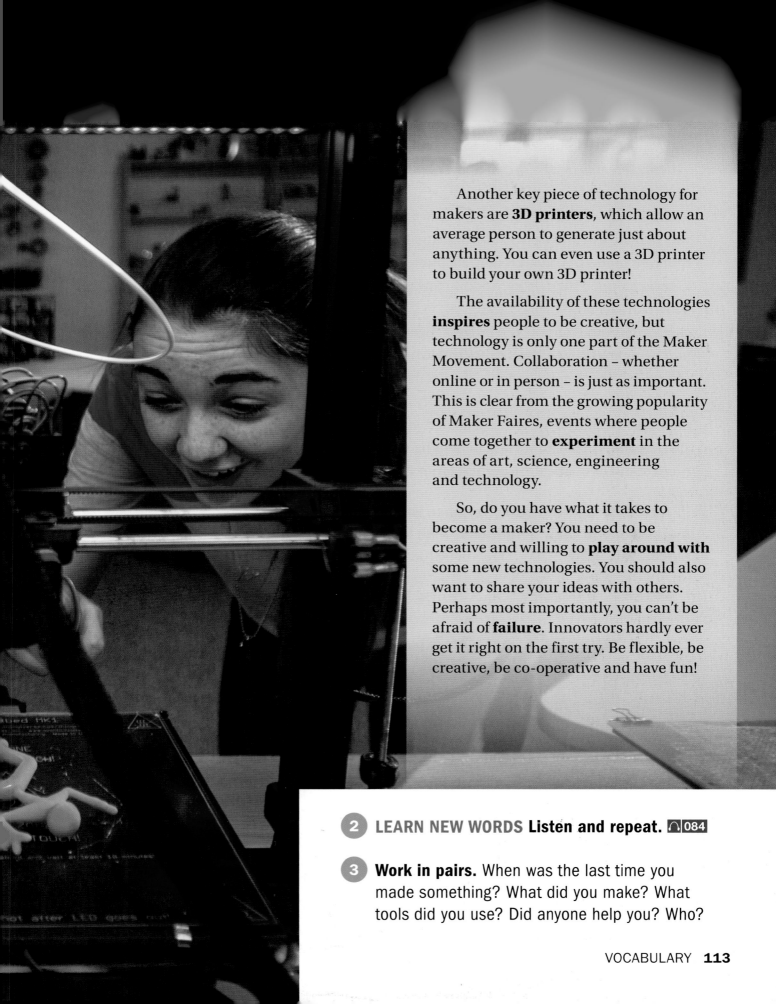

Another key piece of technology for makers are **3D printers**, which allow an average person to generate just about anything. You can even use a 3D printer to build your own 3D printer!

The availability of these technologies **inspires** people to be creative, but technology is only one part of the Maker Movement. Collaboration – whether online or in person – is just as important. This is clear from the growing popularity of Maker Faires, events where people come together to **experiment** in the areas of art, science, engineering and technology.

So, do you have what it takes to become a maker? You need to be creative and willing to **play around with** some new technologies. You should also want to share your ideas with others. Perhaps most importantly, you can't be afraid of **failure**. Innovators hardly ever get it right on the first try. Be flexible, be creative, be co-operative and have fun!

2 **LEARN NEW WORDS Listen and repeat.** 🎧 084

3 **Work in pairs.** When was the last time you made something? What did you make? What tools did you use? Did anyone help you? Who?

4 **Read and write the words from the list.** Make any necessary changes.

| 3D printer | application | concept | device | failure |
| hands-on | inspire | play around with | software | solve |

When entrepreneur Tan Le was a child, she wanted to move objects with her mind. Now she creates headsets that allow people to do just that. The headsets scan our brains and enable us to _____ problems just by thinking about them! Tan's original _____ was to create a _____ that was lightweight and easy to use. She and her team _____ many different models. Although they encountered problems, it never stopped them from working towards their goal. Tan saw both _____ and success as equal parts of the process. Eventually, she and her team created the first wearable brain scanner using EEG, the Emotiv Insight. The headset has a lot of _____ , especially helping people do things with their minds instead of their bodies. The scanner is also important in helping researchers understand how a healthy human brain works.

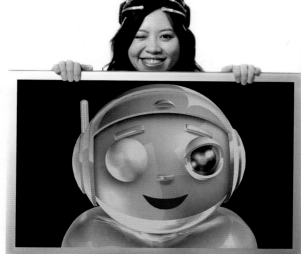

Tan Le uses her mind to control the robot on the screen.

5 **LEARN NEW WORDS Listen to these words and match them to their definitions.** Then listen and repeat. 🎧 085 086

| affordable | approach | flexible | innovator |

_____ 1. not expensive

_____ 2. willing to change or try different things

_____ 3. a person who introduces new ideas

_____ 4. a way of doing something

6 **YOU DECIDE Choose an activity.**

1. **Work independently.** Use the Internet to learn more about do-it-yourself projects. Make a list of five that interest you. Present your favourite project to the class.

2. **Work in pairs.** Survey at least five other students to determine if they are makers. If they are, what do they make? Why? If they aren't, why not? What would they be interested in making? Report your findings to the class.

3. **Work in groups.** Think of a device or app that could solve a problem you have. Does it exist? If so, describe how it works. If not, explain what could be created and how it would help you.

Asking someone to defend an opinion

Why do you think <u>it's important to make things yourself</u>?

Are you sure <u>it's cheaper to make it than to buy it</u>?

What makes you think that?

Can you explain <u>why you think we need to create a device</u>?

So you think <u>the Maker Movement is helping people be more creative</u>?

A 3D printer

1 **Listen.** How does David's mum ask him to defend his opinions? Write the phrases you hear. 🎧 088

2 **Read and complete the dialogue.**

Liz: Dad, look at my biscuit cutter designs. I'm going to print them with the school's 3D printer and then sell them online.

Dad: _____ that will be OK with your school?

Liz: Yes, I'm sure. Actually, it started as a school project, but I think I could really make some money selling them.

Dad: _____ people will buy them?

Liz: Well, my teacher really liked my designs. And my friends have already bought some.

Dad: _____ how you'll do this exactly?

Liz: People could buy the biscuit cutters I have designed and made. Or they could design their own biscuit cutters, and I could print them for them.

Dad: _____ the school will be OK with you using *their* 3D printer for *your* business? _____

Liz: Because it's a learning experience for me – and I'll give the school half the profits!

3 **Work in groups.** On separate strips of paper, write three sentences that give an opinion on technology use. Combine the group's papers into a pile. Take turns reading an opinion and asking the group member who wrote it to defend it.

Today, people spend too much time using smartphones.

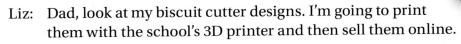
What makes you think that?

4 **Work in pairs.** Think of a problem you have and brainstorm ways that technology can solve it. Discuss your ideas with a partner. Ask your partner to defend his/her opinions when possible.

Wish and **if only**: Expressing wishes and regrets

I wish I were at the technology fair at the moment.

I wish my teacher had told me about the fair before today.

I wish the invitations would go directly to students.

If only we were at the technology fair! We could see a demonstration of the EEG headset.

If only Tan had been invited to our school! She could have shown us her invention here.

1 **Listen.** Listen as the speaker introduces Tan and her Emotiv Insight headset at a technology fair. Select the most logical reaction from each pair, based on what you heard. ∩090

1. **a.** I wish I knew what Tan did.
   b. I wish I could experiment with Tan's headset.

2. **a.** I can't believe the technology is open-source. If only I knew how to use it correctly.
   b. If only the technology were open-source! Then anyone could access it.

3. **a.** I wish Tan would develop ways for disabled people to use the headset.
   b. If only every disabled person had one of these headsets!

4. **a.** If only drivers had used the headset to communicate with each other. Then the accident wouldn't have happened.
   b. If only drivers had used the headset to help them pay attention. Then the accident wouldn't have happened.

5. **a.** I wish I were part of the experiment to have my thoughts 3D printed!
   b. I wish I were a child so that I could get a toy headset.

2 **Work independently.** Listen to the audio again. Imagine that you had an EEG headset for a day. Write sentences expressing wishes and regrets about the experience. ∩091

1. _If only I had been given an EEG headset to_
   keep! I would have shown it to everyone.

2. _____
   _____

3. _____
   _____

3 **Work in pairs.** Rewrite the sentences below to express wishes and regrets.

1. I never learnt to programme computers. *If only I had learnt to programme computers.*

2. My brother doesn't let me use his computer. _____

3. You broke my smartphone. Now we can't play video games! _____

4. My school didn't buy a 3D printer this year. _____

4 **LEARN NEW WORDS Listen to information about an interesting use for EEG headsets.** Then listen and repeat. 🎧 092 093

British musician Daniel Stein, widely known as DJ Fresh, organised the *Mindtunes* project. In it, he helped **disabled** musicians **transform** their thoughts into music. **Wireless** EEG headsets **interpret** signals from their brains. They link these signals to electronic sounds, which the musicians can 'play' with their minds.

5 **Work in pairs.** Write sentences about wishes or regrets using the words provided.

1. interpret my thoughts _____

2. transform into reality _____

3. use a wireless device _____

4. help disabled people _____

6 **Work in groups.** Write two things that you wish you had or could do. Write two things that you wish you had done. Discuss your wishes and regrets with your group.

1. **BEFORE YOU READ Discuss in pairs.** Based on the title and the photos, what do you think you'll learn in this reading?

2. **LEARN NEW WORDS Find these words in the reading.** Use a dictionary to find their meanings. Think of antonyms you know for any of the words. Then listen and repeat. 🎧 094

amount to	discourage	persistent
success	turn away	

3. **WHILE YOU READ Take notes on the failures and successes of the people described.** 🎧 095

4. **AFTER YOU READ Work in pairs to answer the questions.**

1. What did J.K. Rowling think of herself before she became famous?
2. Describe the success of the *Harry Potter* series.
3. What did Albert Einstein's teachers think of him?
4. Why couldn't Einstein find a job after graduation?
5. What was the first electronic device that Masaru Ibuka and Akio Morita made? What was the outcome?
6. What product made their company successful?

5. **Work in pairs.** Using your notes, create a table to categorise the failures and successes of each person described in the text.

You've learnt about Tan Le's incredible innovation, but that didn't come instantly. Tan and her team tried many times before finding success. And Tan's not alone. In fact, for many, success is the result of overcoming great failure.

J.K. Rowling's *Harry Potter* books have sold more than 450 million copies, and have been translated into 77 languages. But before she became famous, Rowling said of herself, 'I was as poor as it is possible to be … I was the biggest failure I knew.' She sent her first book to 12 publishers, but they all rejected it. However, Rowling was persistent. After a year of trying, a publisher finally accepted her manuscript. *Harry Potter and the Philosopher's Stone* became the first novel in a series that would become the best-selling young adult books of all time.

J.K. Rowling

FAILURES

PEOPLE WHO LEARNT TO TRY AND TRY AGAIN

Albert Einstein

When you hear the name Albert Einstein, you probably think *genius*. But many of Einstein's teachers thought he was lazy and wouldn't amount to anything. When he applied to university, he was turned away because he failed the exams. He spent an entire year preparing to re-take them before he was accepted. After graduation, he struggled to get a job because none of his teachers was willing to give him a recommendation. However, Einstein was determined and worked hard. While he worked as a clerk, he continued his studies. He eventually published papers with his theories, and these works changed the field of science. In 1921, Einstein was awarded the Nobel Prize for Physics.

Japanese businessmen Masaru Ibuka and Akio Morita met during World War II. After the war, they started a company repairing radios. When they visited a house to repair a radio, they would receive a bag of rice in addition to payment for their work. This gave them the idea to build and sell rice cookers. Unfortunately, their rice cookers didn't work very well, always over- or under-cooking the rice. But this failure didn't discourage Ibuka and Morita. They continued experimenting with electronics. Their company, Sony®, found success making portable radios. The Walkman® made Sony one of the most successful companies in the world. Today, Sony is known for everything from electronics to films.

These stories show us that failure isn't a sign of losing. In fact, it's part of the process. As Tan says, 'It's like two sides to a coin – you can't have success without failure.'

Akio Morita and Masaru Ibuka

6 **Discuss in groups.**

1. What role did failure play in the success of J.K. Rowling, Albert Einstein, Masaru Ibuka and Akio Morita? What other factors do you think contributed to their successes?

2. How do you deal with failure? Describe a failure you have overcome.

1 BEFORE YOU WATCH **Discuss in groups.**

1. In some parts of the world, children, especially girls, are unable to go to school. Why do you think this is?
2. How would your life be different if you weren't able to go to school?

2 **Work in pairs.** The title of this video is *Sanga's Solution*. It's about energy innovator and National Geographic Explorer Sanga Moses. What do you think it means to be an 'energy innovator'? Predict why Sanga would feel the need to become an energy innovator.

3 WHILE YOU WATCH **Check your prediction from Activity 2.** Watch scene 7.1.

Sanga Moses

4 **AFTER YOU WATCH** **Read the sentences below.** Use the information from the video to decide if each one is *true* or *false*. Tick the correct letter.

1. Sanga had a good job in the city. (T) (F)
2. Sanga's sister was crying because she couldn't go to school. (T) (F)
3. Sanga decided to bring his sister into the city so that she could have a better life. (T) (F)
4. Sanga couldn't quit his job, so he worked on the problem from the city. (T) (F)
5. Sanga was able to solve the problem on his own. (T) (F)
6. Sanga's new company uses waste from agricultural products to create clean fuel. (T) (F)

5 **Work in pairs.** Answer the questions below.

1. What does Sanga's company produce and sell?
2. Who does this product help? How?

6 **Work in groups.** Imagine that you have been asked to sell Sanga's product. Create an advert that advertises at least three benefits to using the product. Share your advert with the class.

7 **YOU DECIDE** **Choose an activity.**

1. **Work independently.** Sanga's idea is an example of 'frugal innovation', or creating something new with very little money or resources. Research other examples of people doing more with less. Share some examples with the class.

2. **Work in pairs.** Compare and contrast Sanga Moses and Tan Le. As innovators, how are they similar? How are they different?

3. **Work in groups.** Do some students regularly miss school in your region? Why is this a problem? What might be a solution? Explain your ideas to the class.

Adverbs: Expressing different levels of intensity

Inventor Kelvin Doe is **so** clever.	But he is **rather** shy.
His inventions work **really** well.	Things changed **kind of** quickly for him.
Kelvin **certainly** knows how to be innovative.	Kelvin can **hardly** wait to share his next invention.

1 **Listen.** Learn about teen inventors. Circle the word that best completes the sentences, based on what you hear. ∩097

1. Kelvin *certainly / sort of* learnt a lot in the United States, but he *hardly / really* wanted to return to his community in Sierra Leone.

2. Deepika Kurup realised that for some people, there was *absolutely / barely* enough clean water to live on, so she created an invention to change that.

3. Kenneth Shinozuka's smart socks have been *kind of / very* important for Alzheimer's patients and their carers.

4. People who suffer from Alzheimer's can *hardly / really* do anything without a carer present.

5. While caring for his family's cows, Richard Turere discovered that the lions that threatened the cows reacted *quite / slightly* negatively to bright, flashing lights.

Deepika Kurup

2 **Work in pairs.** Listen to the information again. Using the words provided, write two additional sentences about the teen inventors. ∩098

1. extremely _____

2. sort of _____

3 **Work in groups.** Cut out the cards and place them in two piles. Choose a card from each pile. Comment on the topic you get using the word on the other card.

It must have been kind of scary for Kenneth to see his grandfather wandering off.

kind of

Kenneth Shinozuka
created sensors to help his grandfather and other Alzheimer's patients.

Go to page 171.

WRITING

When you write an exemplification essay, you present a topic and then use examples to explain it. Well-chosen examples can support your writing by making it more accurate, believable and interesting. Use the following to introduce your examples:

for instance	**a good example is**	**to illustrate**
in particular	**specifically**	**such as**

1 **Read the model.** Work in pairs to identify the parts of the writing. How does the writer signal examples? Underline the phrases.

The other day, while I was at the library, I lost a button on my favourite shirt. I was so upset! It was covered in fabric to match the shirt, so I couldn't replace it. After a few moments of helping me search for the lost button, the librarian asked me if I had clear nail polish. I said I had some at home, so she gave me a tip – cover the buttons on a shirt with clear nail polish and they will stay on better. So I tried it on a different shirt, and it worked!

After learning this trick, I went online to see if there were any other uses for clear nail polish. It turns out there are many. A good example is that clear nail polish can help you thread a needle. Just put a little on the thread, and it will go straight through the eye of a needle.

Of course, clear nail polish is useful for things other than sewing! In particular, it can be used to keep things clean and shiny. For instance, if you paint the bottoms of metal containers with clear nail polish, they won't leave rust stains on your shelf. Put some on your belt buckle or costume jewellery, and it will stay shiny forever. Painting jewellery will also decrease the chance that the jewellery will harm your skin.

You can also use clear nail polish to keep things in place, such as screws. Paint the screw before putting it into the wall, and it will stay in better. Cover a broken piece of wood with clear nail polish, and you won't get splinters. Some people even use clear nail polish to relieve the itch of insect bites!

I don't think I'll use clear nail polish on my nails anymore. It has too many other practical uses!

2 **Work in pairs.** What are the problems that the writer can solve using clear nail polish? Make a list.

3 **Write.** Write an exemplification essay. Name a common problem and describe how an everyday object could be used to solve it.

Don't Give Up

'Part of the process is figuring out what doesn't work as much as what does work.'

Tan Le
National Geographic Explorer, Innovator/Entrepreneur

1. **Watch scene 7.2.**

2. Tan likes to collaborate with others in her work. Do you think it's important to work with others when doing or making new things? How can being part of a team prevent you from quitting or giving up on something?

3. Think of a time when you gave up on something. Why did you give up? What would have happened if you hadn't?

Make an Impact

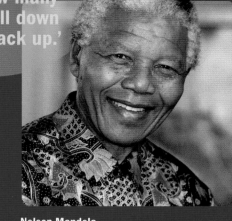

'Do not judge me by my successes, judge me by how many times I fell down and got back up.'

Nelson Mandela

YOU DECIDE Choose a project.

1 Pitch an idea.

- Think of a new idea to solve a problem.

- Create a model or a visual to help explain your idea.

- Pitch your idea to the class. Judges choose the best one.

2 Profile a successful person who has experienced failure.

- Research successful people who have experienced great failures. Choose one to write about.

- Find out about the person's life. Take notes on his/her failures as well as successes.

- Create a profile of this person. Include photos. Present your profile to the class.

'When you lose, you get up, you make it better, you try again.'

Serena Williams

'If I try my best and fail, well, I've tried my best.'

3 Design and advertise your own app.

- Think of a new application for an electronic device.

- Design an example of your app by drawing or creating one or two sample screens. Describe how it will work.

- Create a short advert for your app that would appear online in an app store.

Steve Jobs

Boys looking at art from the *Streets of Afghanistan* exhibition, Afghanistan

Art Connections

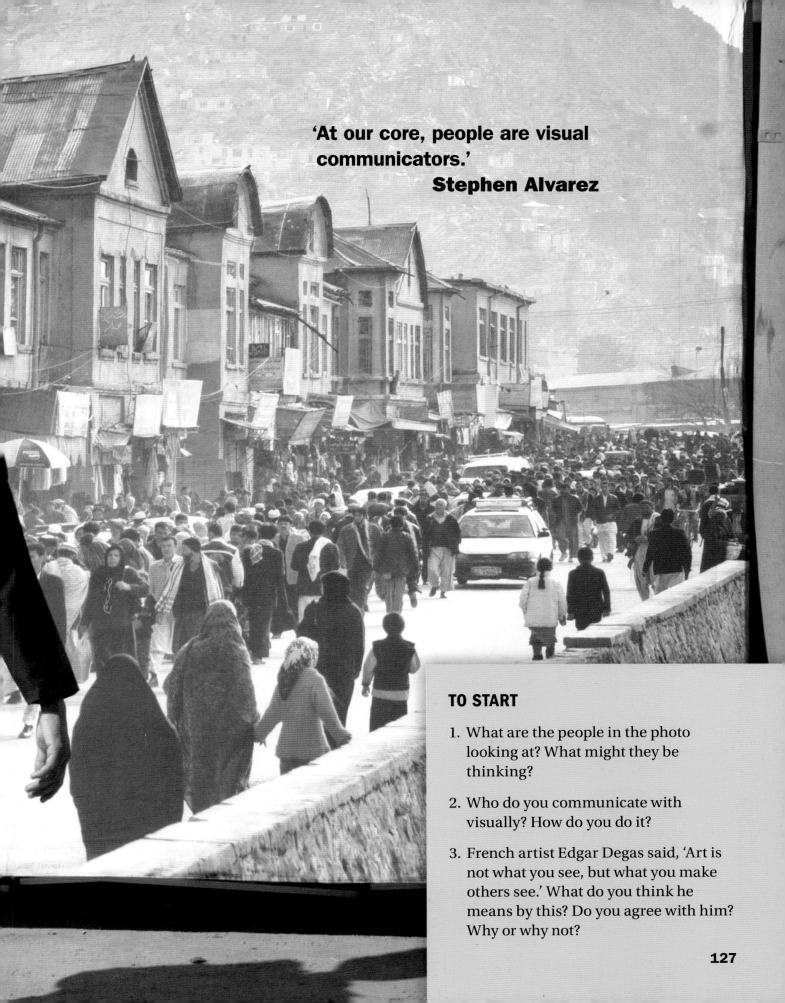

'At our core, people are visual communicators.'
Stephen Alvarez

TO START

1. What are the people in the photo looking at? What might they be thinking?

2. Who do you communicate with visually? How do you do it?

3. French artist Edgar Degas said, 'Art is not what you see, but what you make others see.' What do you think he means by this? Do you agree with him? Why or why not?

Art is part of the human experience. People have **come up with** many reasons to create **artwork** – some simple and others more complex. Art can be purely decorative, or it might be created to generate a certain **reaction**. Art also allows an artist to leave a permanent **mark** on time. A painting or sculpture allows the artist to **preserve** a moment that has long passed.

When did art begin? Well, that's a very **controversial** question. Researchers have been working for decades to **track down** the answer. Some have found triangular drawings on rocks in South Africa that are 75,000 years old. They believe that these triangles are art because they're symbolic of something, though there's no way to know for sure what they represent. Other experts don't think that this finding is that impressive. They argue that the images on the rocks don't **depict** any meaningful message. They suggest that we look to walls, specifically cave walls, to find the origins of art.

Sophisticated paintings from nearly 40,000 years ago have been found in caves in Europe and Asia. A red circle on a wall inside the El Castillo cave in Spain is the oldest known cave art at 40,800 years old. When cave art was first studied in Spain in 1880, researchers felt that it was the **accomplishment** of the earliest humans who migrated from Africa to Europe.

Cave paintings found at Chauvet-Pont-d'Arc in southern France

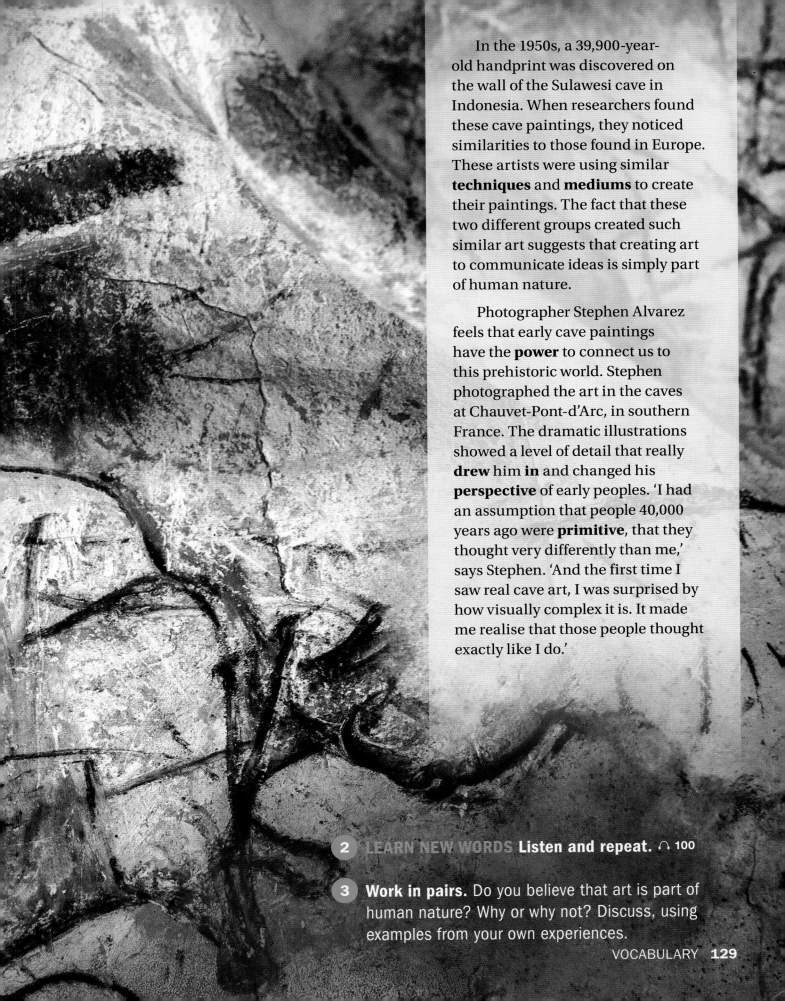

In the 1950s, a 39,900-year-old handprint was discovered on the wall of the Sulawesi cave in Indonesia. When researchers found these cave paintings, they noticed similarities to those found in Europe. These artists were using similar **techniques** and **mediums** to create their paintings. The fact that these two different groups created such similar art suggests that creating art to communicate ideas is simply part of human nature.

Photographer Stephen Alvarez feels that early cave paintings have the **power** to connect us to this prehistoric world. Stephen photographed the art in the caves at Chauvet-Pont-d'Arc, in southern France. The dramatic illustrations showed a level of detail that really **drew** him **in** and changed his **perspective** of early peoples. 'I had an assumption that people 40,000 years ago were **primitive**, that they thought very differently than me,' says Stephen. 'And the first time I saw real cave art, I was surprised by how visually complex it is. It made me realise that those people thought exactly like I do.'

2 LEARN NEW WORDS **Listen and repeat.** ∩ 100

3 **Work in pairs.** Do you believe that art is part of human nature? Why or why not? Discuss, using examples from your own experiences.

4 **Read and write the words from the list.** Make any necessary changes.

accomplishment	artwork	come up with	draw in	medium
power	preserve	reaction	technique	track down

Photography is Stephen Alvarez's preferred _____ for sharing with the rest of us what's hidden underground. As a National Geographic photographer, Stephen travels around the world, and into it, to _____ the best, most powerful images of caves. He has to _____*come*_____ effective _____, such as providing extra lighting, to deal with the challenges of taking photos in such dark areas.

Stephen was really impressed by the _____ on the walls in the Chauvet-Pont-d'Arc cave in France when he photographed it in 2014. He had an incredible _____ to photographing this cave art: a feeling of connection to the artists from 36,000 years ago. 'I wanted to photograph the paintings in a way that let the original artist's voice come through while also _____ the sense of what it is like to stand in front of that art.' Stephen was amazed by the _____ of the art to connect him with these early peoples.

5 **LEARN NEW WORDS Listen to these words and match them to the definitions.** Then listen and repeat. 🎧 101 102

decorative	dramatic	impressive	symbolic

_____ 1. strongly affecting people's emotions

_____ 2. representing something else

_____ 3. useful for making something more attractive

_____ 4. creating a good reaction

6 **YOU DECIDE Choose an activity.**

1. **Work independently.** Go online to find out more about early paintings in one of the caves you read about. Write a paragraph summarising what you learnt. In your conclusion, say whether you were able to connect to the paintings. Explain why or why not.

2. **Work in pairs.** Create a simple drawing or painting that's symbolic of something in your life. Then share it with your partner. See if your partner can guess the meaning of your artwork. When you finish, swap roles.

3. **Work in groups.** Choose a modern mural in your community. Compare it with the cave art pictured on pages 128–129. Consider the medium, technique and meaning of each piece. Summarise the similarities and differences in a short presentation.

Stephen Alvarez photographing ancient art in the Chauvet cave

Interpreting and expressing understanding

Why did early peoples paint these images on the cave's wall?

> Possibly because <u>they didn't have a writing system</u>.
> It seems to me that <u>it was an expression of religious beliefs</u>.
> It appears that <u>there wasn't much else to do for fun</u>.
> Maybe they did it because <u>they wanted to leave a mark</u>.
> Apparently, <u>people wanted to record their experiences</u>.
> This seems to symbolise <u>their interest in the natural world</u>.

Mayan carvings at Holmul, Guatemala, discovered by National Geographic Explorer Francisco Estrada-Belli and his team

1 **Listen.** How do speakers interpret the artwork? Write the words and phrases you hear. 🎧 104

2 **Read and complete the dialogue.**

Carlos: Look at this carved mural, Sylvia. It was discovered in Guatemala. It was preserved in the buried Mayan city of Holmul.

Sylvia: Wow! That's enormous! I wonder why it was so big!

Carlos: _____ the Mayans would usually build new structures on top of older ones, making them bigger.

Sylvia: There are so many different people in the carving. Do you know what they represent?

Carlos: _____ they were Mayan rulers, who were considered gods.

Sylvia: What's that on their heads? Are those birds?

Carlos: Yes. Wearing a headdress made of birds was common in Mayan civilization. They seem to _____ wealth or power.

Sylvia: _____ of all the brightly coloured birds in Guatemala. Their feathers certainly made decorative accessories. And look at this man. Is he holding food?

Carlos: Probably. _____ food was a common offering to the gods.

> It seems to me that the artist had a political message.

3 **Work in groups.** Choose three photos or works of art to share. Put your group's photos into a single pile. Take turns selecting an image from the pile. Then throw the cube. Use the word or phrase on the cube to make a sentence about the image.

Go to page 173.

4 **Work in pairs.** Choose a photo or a piece of artwork in this book and discuss your interpretations of it.

Reported speech: Describing what others say

'This **can't** be an original painting of Georgia O'Keeffe.'	He **argued** that it **couldn't be** an original painting of Georgia O'Keeffe.
'Frida Kahlo **had been injured** in a bus accident. After that, she **began** painting.'	The teacher **explained** that Frida Kahlo **had been injured** in a bus accident and **had begun** painting after that.
'We **will begin** studying sculpture later this year.'	She **pointed out** that they **would begin** studying sculpture later that year.
'Art **should reflect** the world we live in.'	He **suggested** that art **should reflect** the world we live in.
'What exhibition **is** at the art museum this month?'	She **asked** what exhibition **was** at the art museum that month.
'**Go** and see Kobra's murals.' '**You won't** be disappointed!'	They **told us to go** and see Kobra's murals. They **claimed** we **wouldn't** be disappointed.

1 **Read the quotes about art.** Then complete the sentences using reported speech.

'I hate flowers. I paint them because they're cheaper than models and they don't move.'   Georgia O'Keeffe

'I paint flowers so they will not die.' Frida Kahlo

'Treat a work of art like a prince. Let it speak to you first.' Arthur Schopenhauer

'The world today doesn't make sense, so why should I paint pictures that do?' Pablo Picasso

'Art is what you can get away with.' Andy Warhol

'I want to touch people with my art.' Vincent van Gogh

'I don't paint to live, I live to paint.' Willem de Kooning

1. Pablo Picasso stated that _____ ,
   so he wanted to know _____ .

2. Van Gogh explained that _____ .

3. Frida Kahlo reflected that _____ .

4. Georgia O'Keeffe claimed _____ .
   She explained that _____ .

5. Arthur Schopenhauer advised us to _____ .

People all over the world **admire** Eduardo Kobra's murals. **Critics** compliment his **bold** use of colour and attention to detail. Kobra's murals have different **themes**, but many honour the memory of historical figures.

2 **LEARN NEW WORDS Listen to an art teacher's lesson on Brazilian street artist Eduardo Kobra. Then listen and repeat.** 🎧 106 107

3 **Work in pairs.** Listen again to the lesson. Write what the teacher said. Use reported speech and the words provided. 🎧 108

1. say / critics / people walking by
She said that Kobra's first critics were people walking by.

2. point out / street art / accept
_____

3. explain / stand out / bold
_____

4. remind / recognise / subject
_____

5. tell / look at / famous
_____

6. ask / choose / favourite
_____

4 **Work in groups.** Think of a mural in your school or community. Compare it to Eduardo Kobra's mural. Talk about the theme, size, technique, level of detail and use of colour. Then take turns explaining to the class what you discussed.

> We pointed out that Kobra used colours that were much bolder than those on the mural in the cafeteria.

GRAMMAR **133**

Microscopic Marvels

Artist Willard Wigan knows how to make a big impression in small places.

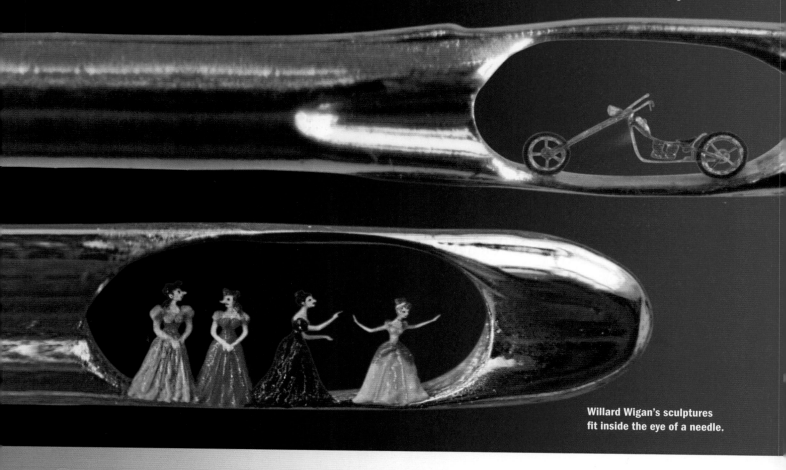

Willard Wigan's sculptures
fit inside the eye of a needle.

1 BEFORE YOU READ Discuss in pairs. Look at the photo on the right. What do you think this man is doing?

2 LEARN NEW WORDS Find these words in the reading. What do you think they mean? Look at the words that appear right before or after each of the words. Then listen and repeat. 🎧 109

detailed	exhibition	honour
miniature	needle	

3 WHILE YOU READ Pause after each paragraph. Write a question you have about Willard Wigan and his work. 🎧 110

4 AFTER YOU READ Work in pairs to respond to the following.

1. Describe the average size of one of Willard's sculptures.
2. How can you see his work?
3. Who buys it?
4. What materials does he use?
5. What were his first micro-sculptures?

'Just because you can't see something, that doesn't mean it's not there.' This old saying is certainly meaningful for British sculptor Willard Wigan. The sculptures he creates are very small, so small that most of them fit on the head of a pin or in the eye of a needle. On average, his works are half the size of the full stop at the end of this sentence.

People from around the world admire Willard's work (through a microscope, of course!). Celebrities and royalty alike own his sculptures. He's even been honoured by the Queen of England for his contributions to the arts. But at every one of his exhibitions, the question is always the same: *How does he do it?*

The answer is very, *very* carefully. So carefully, in fact, that he actually slows his breathing down and works in between breaths. He learnt the hard way that he must do this after he once inhaled one of his sculptures.

Before he begins, Willard collects the materials he needs. Many of his sculptures are made with nylon tags from clothing and fibres found in fabrics and carpets around his house. If fibres are too thick, Willard might instead use pieces of a spider web to add detail. To sculpt, Willard works under a microscope using miniature tools that he creates himself. Amazingly, he rarely uses glue. Instead, he carves spaces into the needle or pin, and forms his work so that it fits into those spaces. To paint his sculptures, Willard uses the hair from a dead fly as a paintbrush.

Creating these detailed works is a very long and difficult process, one that Willard admits isn't always the most enjoyable. 'It's a nightmare when I start but a dream when I finish,' he says. A single sculpture can take up to three months to complete.

People have asked Willard why he has chosen to do something so difficult and time-consuming. His interests in micro-sculpting began when he was five. He started creating houses and playgrounds for ants. Willard was not a strong student. He struggled with dyslexia, and his teachers were quick to call him a failure. This made him feel small, so focusing on little things helped him to feel big. The smaller his work got, the bigger he felt. 'I want to show the world that the little things can be the biggest things,' he says.

5 **Work in pairs.** Share the questions that you wrote in Activity 3. Then discuss their answers. Go online to find any answers that weren't in the reading.

6 **Discuss in groups.**

1. Share your reaction to Willard's work and the process he uses to create it.
2. Go online to find additional photos of his sculptures. Share photos with your group members. Describe which ones you like the best.
3. Willard started creating miniature sculptures because his teachers made him feel small, and he wanted to feel big. What makes you feel small? What can you do to change how you feel in this situation?

1 BEFORE YOU WATCH **Discuss in pairs.**

1. In this video, you will meet National Geographic Photographer Joel Sartore. What do you think you will learn about him?
2. Many of Joel's photos are of animals. What challenges might he face in trying to get good photos? Name at least two.

2 **Write.** The video you're going to watch is called *A Photographer's Life.* List three things that you think are important in a photographer's life.

1. _____

2. _____

3. _____

3 WHILE YOU WATCH **Listen for the traits that Joel says a photographer needs to have.** Circle the traits you hear. Watch scene 8.1.

aggressive	bossy
driven	open-minded
quiet	self-conscious

Joel Sartore with two grizzly bears

4 AFTER YOU WATCH Work in pairs to answer the questions.

1. What does Joel mean when he says, 'you can't sleep on it' (in reference to taking photos)?
2. What does Joel seem to dislike about travelling for work?
3. Why do photographers need to quickly establish friendships in new places?
4. How many photos does Joel shoot each year? How many does he think are worth keeping?
5. What is *The Photo Ark*? How long has Joel been working on it?
6. Why is Joel creating *The Photo Ark*?

5 Work in pairs. Joel wants people to 'look these species in the eye so that they care about these animals more'. Why would eye contact make us care more? How do you think eye contact affects relationships between people? Does eye contact have the same effect between animals and people? Explain.

6 Work in groups. In the video, Joel says, 'Most species are going extinct because we don't pay any attention to them.' Give two or three examples of this. Discuss ways to raise awareness of these animals.

7 YOU DECIDE Choose an activity.

1. **Work independently.** Photograph an animal on a plain black or white surface. Show the photo to the class. Say how and where you took it. Was it easy or difficult? Describe any challenges you faced.

2. **Work in pairs.** Research Joel's project *The Photo Ark*. Choose your favourite five photos. Present them to the class, describing each of the animals.

3. **Work in groups.** Compare and contrast the photography of Joel Sartore and Stephen Alvarez (or another famous photographer). How is their work different? What is the same? Create a Venn diagram to show your comparison.

Two- and three-word verbs

Separable

Artists want to **draw in** their viewers.
Artists want to **draw** their viewers **in**.
Artists want to **draw** us **in**.

I'm working to **track down** the origins of art.
I'm working to **track** the origins of art **down**.
I'm working to **track** them **down**.

Can we **work out** the meaning of this painting?
Can we **work** the meaning **out**?
Can we **work** it **out**?

Inseparable

A true artist **comes up with** unique ways to express herself.

Critics **rave about** the modern art exhibition at the museum. They say it's really impressive!

I'm **looking forward to** seeing the works on display.

Self-Portrait with Bandaged Ear by Vincent van Gogh, 1889

1 **Read and complete the sentences.** Make any necessary changes. For help, see pages 149–152.

come up with	cut off	get away with	look down on
look forward to	take down	track down	work out

1. Vincent van Gogh suffered mental illness, which led him to _____ his ear _____ .

2. Andy Warhol says that 'Art is what you can _____ .'

3. Author Robert Edsel is working to _____ works of art that were lost during World War II.

4. One family _____ a Diego Rivera painting _____ and destroyed it because they didn't like the political message.

5. Wealthy Japanese art buyers _____ the technique of woodblock printing used by Katsushika Hokusai. They didn't like making art so accessible.

2 **Work in groups.** Research information for each of the categories on the game board. Then choose a topic and a verb. Make sentences with the information you researched.

> The Statue of Liberty was supposed to be in Egypt, but instead it ended up in the United States.

	Painting	Famous Artists	Cave Art	Sculpture	Abstract Art
100	FREE	cut off	stand out	fit in	work out

Go to page 175.

WRITING

In an art review, you need to give both facts and opinions. Research the artwork and its artist to help you understand the work and the context it was created in. In your review, answer the following questions:

· **What do you see?**

· **How did the artist create the work?**

· **Why did the artist create the work?**

· **What is your reaction to the work?**

1 **Read the model.** Underline the answers to each of the questions above.

The Great Wave off Kanagawa is one of the best-known pieces of art in the world. Japanese artist Katsushika Hokusai created the image sometime around 1830. It was part of a series of 36 images to feature Mount Fuji, Japan's highest mountain. In this image, Mount Fuji is far off in the background and looks very small from the viewer's perspective. Fishing boats and their crews are being thrown around by the enormous waves, and viewers can only hope that they get out of the sea unharmed.

The series of images that includes *The Great Wave off Kanagawa* was created on wood blocks. To create the work, Hokusai first drew the image with ink and then carved it into the wood. Next, coloured ink was put on the blocks. Sheets of paper were then pressed onto each of the blocks to print the design. Because Hokusai used this technique to create multiple copies, many people could own this print.

Hokusai had been painting for years before creating this famous print. In fact, he was in his seventies when it came out. He probably chose to feature Mount Fuji because it is considered a sacred place in Japan. The print method was good for selling art, which may have been another reason why Hokusai created the series.

The Great Wave off Kanagawa is an excellent example of Japanese art. It draws viewers in with its exaggerated movement and interesting perspective. Hokusai uses both Japanese and Western techniques, which give the print a unique style. This also makes the art accessible so that, even today, people everywhere can connect with 19th century Japan.

2 **Work in pairs.** What is the author's opinion of the artwork? Do you agree? Why or why not?

3 **Write.** Write a review of a piece of artwork that you've seen in this unit or elsewhere. Make sure you research the work. Include facts and opinions in your review.

NATIONAL GEOGRAPHIC

Connect Through Art

'We use art as a way to bind society together.'

Stephen Alvarez
National Geographic Photographer

1. **Watch scene 8.2.**

2. Stephen says that art is a way to 'bind society', or connect people together. Think of an example of public art in your community. How does it bring people together?

3. Even if you don't create your own art, you can use art to connect with others. List three ways you can do this.

Make an Impact

YOU DECIDE Choose a project.

① **Hold an art auction.**

· Choose three pieces of art to bring to class.

· Prepare a short description of each piece of art. Talk about the artist, the context in which the artwork was created and its connection to modern life.

· Hold an art auction for your class. Display each piece and describe it. Try to sell each item to the highest bidder.

Still Life with Apples by Paul Cézanne, 1894

② **Create an art book.**

· Research artwork and quotations about artwork. Select five of each.

· Compile the artwork and quotations into a decorative art book.

· Present your book to the class. As you share, explain your connection to the artwork and the quotations.

The Houses of Parliament, Sunset by Claude Monet, 1903

③ **Re-create cave art.**

· Choose a cave that you have learnt about in this unit, or another cave with prehistoric paintings.

· Research the specific images found on the cave wall. Learn about the medium and the technique used.

· Recreate this art on a piece of cardboard. Present your artwork to the class. Explain what it represents and how you did it. Compare the process to that of the original artists.

Concert of Birds, Circle of Jan van Kessel (Anonymous), 1660/1670

Express Yourself

1 Read and listen to information about a contest and an entry to the contest. 🎧 112

Droidganiser

Submitted by Alexandra Poulos, age 16

Like most people my age, I hate tidying my room. My mum always tells me that if I don't like doing it, I can save my money to buy a robot that will tidy for me. She's joking, of course, but her joke gave me an idea. What if I really *could* get a robot to tidy my room?

As a member of my school's robotics club, I'm learning that it might actually be possible to make, not buy, this robot. My idea, *Droidganiser*, would build on technological devices that already exist to help around the house. Currently, there are robotic devices that vacuum and mop the floor using sensors to control their movement. Robots also have the ability to pick things up with robotic limbs. *Droidganiser* would combine these applications into a single device.

What would really set *Droidganiser* apart from current devices is its monitor. A *Droidganiser* owner would put the monitor on the ceiling somewhere in the room. The person would clean and tidy the room the first time and then use the monitor to take a photo of how the room should look. The monitor would store this information. Then it would monitor the room from the ceiling. Whenever the room doesn't match the photo, *Droidganiser* would automatically fix the problem. It would pick up clothes or books on the floor and put them away. It might also make the bed. *Droidganiser* could even be programmed to vacuum, dust or clean the windows!

Anyone would be happy to have a *Droidganiser* to do the dirty work. If only *Droidganiser* existed now! People could be using their time to study, play sports or hang out with friends – not cleaning!

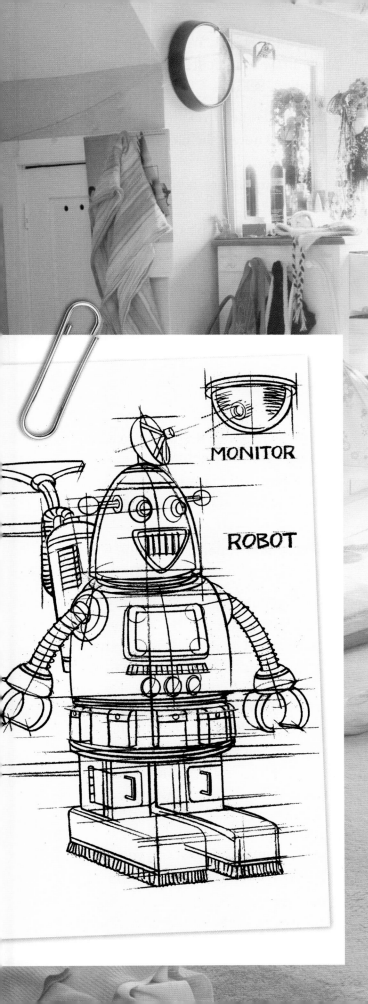

MONITOR

ROBOT

2 **Discuss in pairs.**

1. You just read about a device that would solve a problem. Do you think the concept presented is unique? Should Alexandra's entry be considered for the contest? Explain.

2. What steps do you think are involved in inventing and selling a product like *Droidganiser*? List at least five. Then compare your list with another pair.

3. Why do you think the contest organisers asked for a design? How can the design be useful in helping them connect with the idea?

3 **Connect ideas.** In Unit 7, you learnt about creative problem-solving. In Unit 8, you learnt about art connections. What connection do you see between the two units?

4 **YOU DECIDE** **Choose an activity.**

1. Choose a topic:
   • creative problem-solving
   • art connections

2. Choose a way to express yourself:
   • a magazine article
   • an entry for an art or technology contest
   • a short video

3. Present your work.

Unit 1

Intonation in embedded *yes/no* questions

1 **Listen.** Notice how the voice falls at the end of the statement and rises at the end of a question with a *yes* or *no* answer. 🎧 113

Statement: Cory Richards is a photographer.

Yes/No question: Is Cory a climber?

If a *yes/no* question is embedded, however, the intonation depends *not* on the question, but on the sentence with the embedded question. If the sentence is a statement, the voice falls at the end. If it's a *yes/no* question, the voice rises at the end.

I wonder <u>if Cory is a climber</u>.

Do you know <u>if Cory is a climber</u>?

2 **Listen and repeat.** Write an up or down arrow to indicate the final intonation. 🎧 114

1. I wonder if he's ever surfed. _____
2. Do you know if she has a role model? _____
3. I'm not sure if he's achieved a goal. _____
4. Are you asking if he's reached his limit? _____

3 **Work in pairs.** Take turns completing the two embedded questions for each item using *I wonder if he/she ...* and *Do you know if he/she ... ?*

I wonder if she's <u>ever surfed</u>.   Do you know if she's <u>ever surfed</u>?

1. Has she ever surfed?
2. Does he have a hobby?
3. Does she take many risks?
4. Has he overcome an obstacle?

Unit 2

Stress in compound nouns

1 **Listen.** Notice the stress in these compound nouns. 🎧 115

A *compound noun* is formed when two words come together to form a single noun.

crowdsourcing   **earth**quake
mobile phone   **fund**raiser
text message   **sea** level

The first word in most compound nouns receives the main stress. This differs from adjective + noun combinations, where the second word usually receives the main stress.

This is a good **phone**.   What's the best **date**?
This is a **mobile** phone.   What's the **up**date?

2 **Listen and repeat.** Circle the word with the main stress. 🎧 116

1. a **lap**top   5. a nice top
2. a loud call   6. a phone call
3. the hard work   7. the homework
4. daytime   8. good time

3 **Work in pairs.** Take turns reading the clues aloud. For each clue, your partner will say the compound noun.

work you do at home   **home**work

1. work you do at home
2. a computer that sits on your lap
3. another student from your class
4. a room where you sleep
5. food from the ocean

Unit 3

The *ar* sound

1 **Listen.** Notice the pronunciation of the letter *a* in the word *demand*. 🎧 117

*Insects are a good solution to the increased dem**a**nd for protein.*

In English, the letter *a* is sometimes pronounced like an *ar* sound. This is called a *long vowel sound*. Listen again.

Listen to the examples.

f**a**ther   gr**a**ss   ex**a**mple

2 **Work in pairs.** Listen to these words. Circle the ones that contain the *ar* sound. 🎧 118

1. demand
2. tomato
3. potato
4. sandwich
5. plant

3 **Listen to the sentences.** Complete them with the correct words. Then listen and check. 🎧 119

1. _____ for new sources of protein is increasing.
2. His _____ was a famous chef.
3. The archaeologist discovered a gold burial _____ .
4. Would you like to come to the _____ on Saturday night?
5. There have been many scientific _____ during the _____ century.

Unit 4

Expressing emotions with intonation

1 **Listen.** Notice the different possible emotions in the responses. 🎧 120

A: There's a new amusement park nearby!
B1: That's great! (enthusiastic/excited)
B2: That's great. (sarcastic/annoyed/not interested)
B3: That's great? (questioning/doubtful)

Speakers use intonation in various ways to express emotions. Listen again. Notice how the voice is sometimes higher and sometimes lower.

Generally, a speaker's voice becomes higher when the speaker is positive (happy, excited, enthusiastic) and lower when negative (angry, annoyed, sarcastic).

2 **Listen.** Circle the responses with an excited emotion. 🎧 121

1. —The Olympics will be here.   —Fantastic.
2. —The water is recycled.   —That's great.
3. —I got you a ticket to the park.   —Thank you.
4. —Look at that roller coaster.   —Wow.
5. —He became president.   —Interesting.

> The Olympics will be here!   Fantastic!

3 **Work in pairs.** Take turns saying the sentences in Activity 2. Respond with one of the two emotions. Circle your partner's emotion.

1. Awesome.   a. sarcastic   b. excited
2. That's great.   a. questioning   b. enthusiastic
3. Thank you.   a. annoyed   b. questioning
4. Wow.   a. sarcastic   b. excited
5. Interesting.   a. excited   b. doesn't care

Unit 5

Sounds of letter x

1 **Listen.** Notice the pronunciation of the letter x. 🎧 122

ks	gz
ex**plore**	ex**act**
Mexico	ex**ist**

The letter x can be pronounced two ways – *ks* or *gz*. The pronunciation is usually *ks*. However, when the x comes before a vowel **and** the syllable after x is stressed, the x sounds like *gz*.

Note: There are a few words that begin with x (*xylophone*). In this case, the x sounds like *z*.

2 **Listen and repeat.** Then write *ks* or *gz* to indicate the sound of x. 🎧 123

1. __ks__ explore
2. _____ expert
3. _____ executive
4. _____ exercise
5. _____ exam
6. _____ complex
7. _____ exist
8. _____ exactly

3 **Work in pairs.** Complete the paragraph with the words. Then listen and check your answers. Take turns reading the paragraph with your partner. 🎧 124

> exactly   exciting   existence   expedition   experience
>
> explore   Mexican   Mexico   taxes

Come and ___explore___ _____ ! Our _____ is led by an _____ in _____ history. In your fascinating ten-day _____ , you will learn about the _____ of prehistoric civilizations.

The cost of this _____ trip is _____ €3,000. No _____ or added fees. Book today!

Unit 6

Pausing: Relative clauses

1 **Listen.** Notice the pauses in these relative clauses. 🎧 125

Dinosaurs,/ **which were reptiles,**/ are the ancestors of birds.

Reptiles **that flew in prehistoric times** were not dinosaurs.

Herbivores,/ **which don't eat meat,**/ can be very large animals.

An animal **that eats meat** is a carnivore.

In writing, commas often indicate a pause. If the relative clause does not have a comma, there's no pause.

2 **Listen and repeat.** Add a comma if you hear a pause before and after the relative clause. 🎧 126

1. Elephants and moose, **which are herbivores,** are large land animals.
2. The moose **that ran in front of the car** is OK.
3. Catalina Pimiento **who is a scientist** studies sharks.
4. Great white sharks scare people **who swim or surf.**
5. Nizar Ibrahim studies *Spinosaurus* **which was a prehistoric river monster.**

3 **Listen.** Notice the pauses. Listen again and read the sentences with the speaker. 🎧 127

1. *Spinosaurus*, which lived around 97 million years ago, was huge. It had massive teeth that were razor sharp.
2. *T. rex*, which many believe was the largest dinosaur, was smaller than *Spinosaurus*. *T. rex* had a long tail that was very heavy.

Unit 7
Variations in stress and intonation

1 **Listen.** Notice the stress and intonation differences in the pair of sentences. 🎧 **128**

The invention is **really great**.

The invention is **really great**.

The stress on the adverb ***really*** is stronger in the second example. The speaker emphasises it to express a stronger belief. The vowel is longer, and the speaker's voice rises.

Speakers also emphasise words when:

- contrasting information
- correcting information
- stating new information

2 **Listen and repeat.** Circle the syllable with stronger emphasis. 🎧 **129**

1. **Wow. This drone flies (so) high**.
2. **Wow. This drone flies so high**.
3. A: It was a **great** idea.
   B: It was an **awful** idea.
4. A: **Jane won** the **science con**test.
   B: **Tim won** the **science con**test.
5. A: You **love** ro**bo**tics?
   B: Yes, **micro**-ro**bo**tics.

3 **Work in pairs.** Take turns saying the sentences in Activity 2. Discuss the meaning of the special emphasis in each sentence or dialogue.

Wow. This **drone flies SO high**.

The speaker can't believe how high the drone flies. It's very high.

Unit 8
Stress with two- and three-word verbs

1 **Listen.** Notice the stress in these sentences. 🎧 **130**

I **worked out** the **mean**ing.

I **worked** the **mean**ing **out**.

I **worked** it **out**.

In separable two-word verbs, both words are stressed. The object is also stressed except when it's a pronoun.

Notice the stress in these sentences.

She **puts up** with the **noise**.

She **puts up** with it.

In three-word verbs, the third word (*with*) is a preposition. Prepositions are not usually stressed. The first two words as well as the object are stressed, unless the object is a pronoun.

2 **Listen and repeat.** Tap your finger as you say the stressed syllables. 🎧 **131**

1. I can't **work out** the **mean**ing.
2. A: She **came up** with a **great idea**.
   B: How did she **come up** with it?
3. A: Did you **track down** the **own**ers?
   B: No, I couldn't **track** them **down**.
4. A: Why did van Gogh **cut** his **ear off**?
   B: I didn't know that he **cut** it **off**.

3 **Work in pairs.** Listen and repeat these questions. Then ask and answer them with your partner. 🎧 **132**

Who **cut off** his **ear**?

Van Gogh.

1. Who **cut off** his **ear**?
2. If your friends are sad, how do you **cheer** them **up**?
3. What do you use to **look up** infor**ma**tion?
4. What is something that you **look for**ward to?

Irregular Verbs

Infinitive	Past simple	Past participle	Infinitive	Past simple	Past participle
be	were	been	leave	left	left
beat	beat	beaten	lend	lent	lent
become	became	become	let	let	let
begin	began	begun	lie (down)	lay	lain
bend	bent	bent	light	lit	lit
bet	bet	bet	lose	lost	lost
bite	bit	bitten	make	made	made
bleed	bled	bled	mean	meant	meant
blow	blew	blown	meet	met	met
break	broke	broken	overcome	overcame	overcome
bring	brought	brought	pay	paid	paid
build	built	built	put	put	put
burn	burnt	burnt	quit	quit	quit
buy	bought	bought	read	read	read
carry	carried	carried	ride	rode	ridden
catch	caught	caught	ring	rang	rung
choose	chose	chosen	rise	rose	risen
come	came	come	run	ran	run
cost	cost	cost	say	said	said
cut	cut	cut	see	saw	seen
deal	dealt	dealt	sell	sold	sold
dig	dug	dug	send	sent	sent
dive	dived	dived	set	set	set
do	did	done	sew	sewed	sewn
draw	drew	drawn	shake	shook	shaken
drink	drank	drunk	shine	shone	shone
drive	drove	driven	show	showed	shown
dry	dried	dried	shrink	shrank	shrunk
eat	ate	eaten	shut	shut	shut
fall	fell	fallen	sing	sang	sung
feed	fed	fed	sink	sank	sunk
feel	felt	felt	sit	sat	sat
fight	fought	fought	sleep	slept	slept
find	found	found	slide	slid	slid
flee	fled	fled	speak	spoke	spoken
fly	flew	flown	spend	spent	spent
forbid	forbade	forbidden	spin	spun	spun
forget	forgot	forgotten	stand	stood	stood
forgive	forgave	forgiven	steal	stole	stolen
freeze	froze	frozen	stick	stuck	stuck
fry	fried	fried	sting	stung	stung
get	got	got	stink	stank	stunk
give	gave	given	strike	struck	struck
go	went	gone	swear	swore	sworn
grind	ground	ground	sweep	swept	swept
grow	grew	grown	swim	swam	swum
hang	hung	hung	swing	swung	swung
have	had	had	take	took	taken
hear	heard	heard	teach	taught	taught
hide	hid	hidden	tear	tore	torn
hit	hit	hit	tell	told	told
hold	held	held	think	thought	thought
hurt	hurt	hurt	throw	threw	thrown
keep	kept	kept	understand	understood	understood
kneel	knelt	knelt	wake	woke	woken
knit	knitted	knitted	wear	wore	worn
know	knew	known	weave	wove	woven
lay	laid	laid	win	won	won
lead	led	led	write	wrote	written

Two-word verbs – Inseparable

Verb	Meaning	Sample sentence
amount to	be the same as; turn out to be	The total **amounts to** five hundred. Some people thought he would not **amount to** anything, but he became famous.
apply for	to make a request	Do you plan to **apply for** a summer job?
apply to	be relevant	The rules **apply to** everyone!
ask around	ask several people	I'll **ask around** in case anyone found a lost phone.
break down	stop functioning	The car **broke down** yesterday.
break up	end a relationship	Did you hear that Lara and Renato **broke up**?
calm down	relax after being angry	**Calm down**! Everything will be OK.
check in	register at a hotel or airport	We can't **check in** until one o'clock.
check out	leave a hotel	He **checked out** at 10.20 and went straight to the airport.
cheer up	become happier	**Cheer up**! I'm sure your team will do better next time.
come across	find unexpectedly	I **came across** a very interesting article about crocodiles.
come from	originate in	Mangoes originally **come from** Asia.
count on	rely on	Please be there on time. I'm **counting on** you!
dress up	wear nice clothes	Mum, do I really need to **dress up** for the party?
eat out	eat at a restaurant	Why don't we **eat out** on Friday?
end up	eventually do/decide	We **ended up** going to the cinema last night.
engage in	take part in	The head teacher **engaged in** talks with the student council.
fall apart	break into pieces	Mum, I need a new desk. This one's **falling apart**.
fall down	fall to the ground	The vase **fell down** and smashed.
find out	learn	I was so excited when I **found out** we were going to Spain!
fit in	blend in; belong because you're similar	Teenagers wear certain clothes to **fit in**.
get along	be friendly with someone	I really like Tom. We **get along** well.
get over	recover from a problem	I know she's upset you didn't call her, but she'll **get over** it.
get together	meet; gather	Let's **get together** on Wednesday after school!
get up	get out of bed; rise	I **get up** at seven o'clock every day.
give in	surrender; quit	I won't **give in** to pressure from my friends.
give up	stop trying	This puzzle is really hard, but we won't **give up**!
go ahead	do; begin to do	Why don't you **go ahead** and invite her to the party?
go back	return	He **went back** to the site and discovered a second dinosaur.
go over	review	Let's **go over** the presentation before the lesson.
grow up	become an adult	I **grew up** in China.
hang in	stay positive	**Hang in** there. I'm sure you'll find the phone.
hang on	wait	**Hang on** a minute. I'm on the phone.
hang out	spend time	Do you want to **hang out** on Saturday?
hold on	wait	**Hold on** a second! I think I found the answer.
lead to	cause to happen	His research **led to** the discovery of a new species.

Verb	Meaning	Sample sentence
light up	become bright	The sky **lit up** with fireworks.
log in/on	sign in to a website or app	I can't **log in** because I can't remember my password.
look after	take care of	I have to **look after** my little sister on Sunday.
look back	think about things that happened in the past	**Looking back,** I think the other project topic was more interesting.
look for	try to find	What are you **looking for**? Did you lose something?
look into	try to find out about	I need to **look into** it. I'll let you know tomorrow.
not care for	not like	I do**n't** really **care for** opera.
pass away	die	I heard Kim's grandma **passed away**.
prey on	hunt and kill for food	Do lions **prey on** zebras?
rave about	talk or write very enthusiastically	Critics are **raving about** the new film.
rely on	trust; depend on	Do you think we **rely on** technology too much?
run away	escape; leave	Our dog **ran away**!
run into	meet unexpectedly; collide	Yesterday I **ran into** my old teacher. I **ran into** a tree.
stand out	be noticeable	I was the only one wearing purple. I really **stood out**.
take off	start to fly	The flight **took off** on time.
turn out	result; happen	I thought everyone in my family had a mobile phone. It **turns out** my uncle refuses to get one!
wake up	stop sleeping	I usually **wake up** at six o'clock.
warm up	prepare for exercise	Do you **warm up** before football games?
work out	be successful; exercise	Everyone liked our presentation. It **worked out** well! I prefer to **work out** in the gym when it's cold.

Two-word verbs – Separable

Verb	Meaning	Sample sentence
back up	support	His friends **backed** him **up**.
call off	cancel	They had planned a party, but they had to **call** it **off**.
calm down	help relax	Let's play soft music to **calm** the baby **down**.
carry out	do or complete something	They are **carrying out** research on ancient birds.
check out	observe; notice	**Check out** my new phone!
cheer up	try to make someone happy	Why don't we get some flowers to **cheer** her **up**?
clean up	organise; clean	Can you **clean** that **up**? Guests are arriving soon.
cut down	make something fall to the ground	They're **cutting down** too many trees.
cut off	remove by cutting	Did you read about that hiker that had to **cut off** his own arm?
draw in	capture the interest	This book really **drew** me **in**.
equip with	supply with	They **equipped** the astronauts **with** extra oxygen tanks.
fill out/in	write information in a form	Remember to **fill out** the form before the end of the week. **Fill in** your details on page 6.

Verb	Meaning	Sample sentence
fill up	fill to the top	Don't **fill up** the cup. I need room for milk.
find out	discover information	How did you **find** that **out**?
get across	make understandable	We need to add more examples to **get** the idea **across**!
give back	return something	Have you still got my book? Can you **give** it **back** to me?
give up	stop (a habit)	I'm **giving up** coffee!
hand in	submit	Did you **hand in** your homework on time?
hand out	distribute	I'll make copies and **hand** them **out**.
let down	disappoint	I really want you to come to the party. Don't **let** me **down**.
let in	allow to come in	They didn't **let** him **in** with his rucksack.
light up	make bright	At night the stars **light** the sky **up**.
look up	find information	Can you **look** it **up** in a dictionary?
make up	lie about; invent	That can't be true. I think he **made** it **up**.
mix up	confuse things or people	They always **mix** me **up** with my sister.
put off	postpone	Can we **put off** the meeting until next week?
put together	assemble	Can you help me **put** this **together**?
take down	remove	They **took down** the painting because it was controversial.
take off	remove	**Take off** that coat. You'll be too hot.
take over	gain control of	He **took over** the company when his father died.
throw away	put in the rubbish; get rid of	Don't **throw away** plastic bottles. Recycle them.
track down	find after a long search	I'm trying to **track down** a friend from my childhood.
try on	put on to see if it fits	I **tried on** my sister's shoes, but they didn't fit.
turn away	reject; refuse to admit	Hundreds of people were **turned away** from the audition.
turn down	decrease the strength	**Turn** the TV **down** a bit. It's too loud.
turn off	power off	Don't forget to **turn off** the lights when you leave.
turn on	power on	**Turn on** the TV. The match has started!
turn up	increase the strength	I can't hear. Can you **turn up** the volume?
warm up	make warmer	Can you **warm up** the milk?
work out	find a solution	I'm sure you'll **work** it **out**.

Three-word verbs – Inseparable

Verb	Meaning	Sample sentence
add up to	become a certain amount; result in something	The total **adds up to** two hundred.
break up with	end a relationship	She **broke up with** her boyfriend last week.
come down with	become ill	He **came down with** a cold.
come up against	face; confront	He **came up against** many obstacles during his research.
come up with	think of; find a solution	She **came up with** an excellent plan.
cut down on	use less of; do less	You should **cut down on** your screen time!
get along with	be friendly with	My sister **gets along with** everyone!
get round to	find time to finally do	I finally **got round to** writing my blog.
get away with	not get caught	How did you **get away with** not doing your homework?
get back into	become interested again	I stopped playing football two years ago, but then I **got back into** it.

Verb	Meaning	Sample sentence
get out of	avoid doing something you don't want to do	I think that's just an excuse to **get out of** doing the project!
give up on	lose hope that somebody or something will succeed	I **gave up on** trying to become an athlete.
grow out of	change your mind over time; become too big for	He wants to be a rock star, but I'm sure he'll **grow out of** it. You'll **grow out of** that jacket before winter is over!
look down on	feel that somebody is less important	Many people **looked down on** him and his art, but he went on to become a famous artist.
look forward to	be excited about (something in the future)	I **look forward to** going on holiday.
look out for	protect; take care of	He's very selfish! He only **looks out for** himself.
look up to	have a lot of respect for	Many youngsters **look up to** athletes or pop stars.
play around with	try several options	I **played around with** it until I found the problem!
put up with	tolerate	Our teacher doesn't **put up with** bad behaviour.
run out of	use everything	I think we've **run out of** milk. Can you get some?
stand up for	defend	Don't let him make fun of you. **Stand up for** yourself!
watch out for	be alert; anticipate	**Watch out for** deer crossing the road!

Verbs followed by infinitives and gerunds

Verbs followed by infinitive			Verbs followed by infinitive or noun/pronoun + infinitive		Verbs followed by noun/pronoun + infinitive	
He **agreed to go.**			He **wants to learn** French. I **want him to learn** French.		I **convinced her to try** sushi.	
afford	deserve	offer	ask	prepare	cause	motivate
agree	fail	plan	choose	promise	challenge	order
appear	happen	pretend	dare	want	convince	persuade
arrange	hesitate	refuse	expect	wish	empower	remind
attempt	hope	seem	need	would like	forbid	tell
care	intend	tend			force	urge
claim	learn	vow			hire	warn
decide	manage	wait			invite	
demand						

Verbs followed by gerund or noun/pronoun + infinitive	Verbs followed by a gerund				
They don't **allow surfing** here. They didn't **allow him to surf** here.	You should **avoid swimming** there.				
advise	admit	delay	imagine	mind	report
allow	anticipate	deny	involve	miss	resist
encourage	appreciate	discuss	justify	postpone	risk
permit	avoid	dislike	keep	practise	suggest
require	can't help	enjoy	look forward to	put off	understand
	carry on	feel like	mention	recommend	
	consider	finish			

Verbs followed by infinitive or gerund (similar meaning)			Verbs followed by infinitive or gerund (different meaning)	
I **hate waking** up early. I **hate to wake** up early.			I **remember going** there last year. I **remembered to go** to the shop.	
begin	hate	prefer	forget	remember
can't bear	like	propose	go on	stop
can't stand	love	start	quit	try
continue			regret	

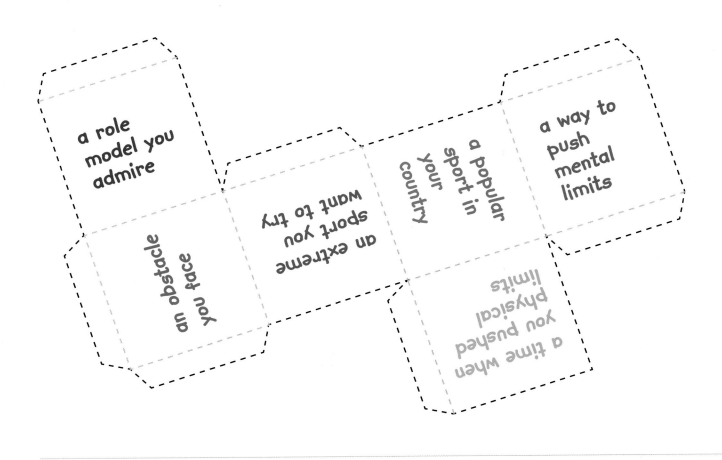

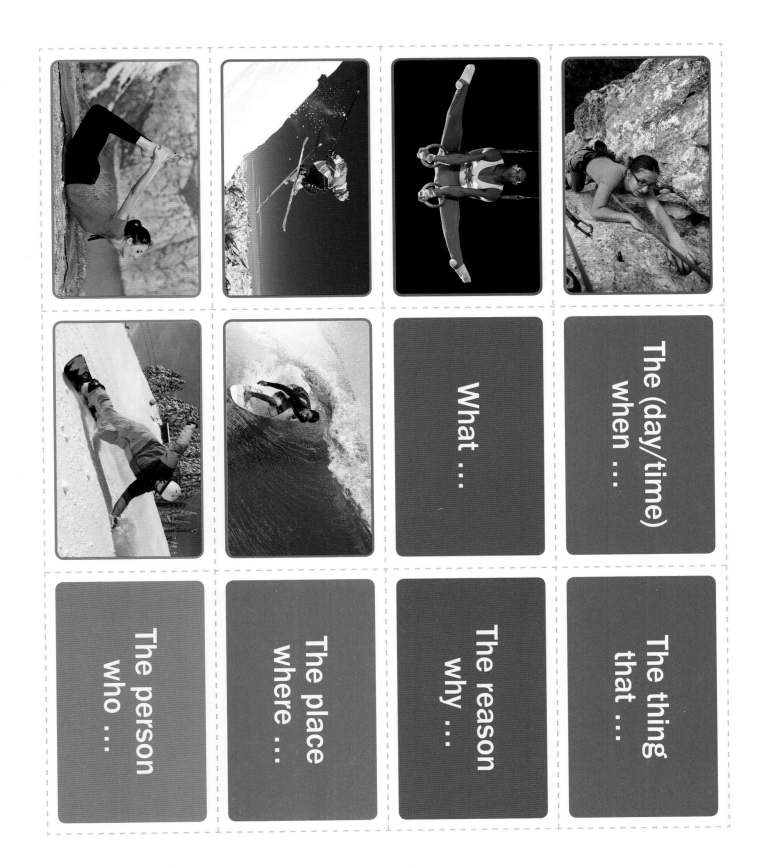

What ...

The (day/time) when ...

The person who ...

The place where ...

The reason why ...

The thing that ...

	Technology	People	The world	School	Transport
100	computers	live	people	homework	bicycles
200	television	buy	country	classrooms	cars
300	mobile phones	work	environment	computers	aeroplanes
400	games	have	population	teachers	space travel
500	radio	eat	problem	classes	trains

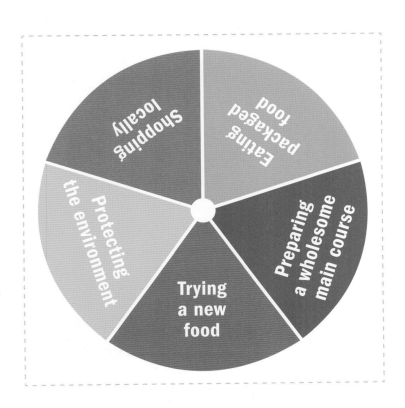

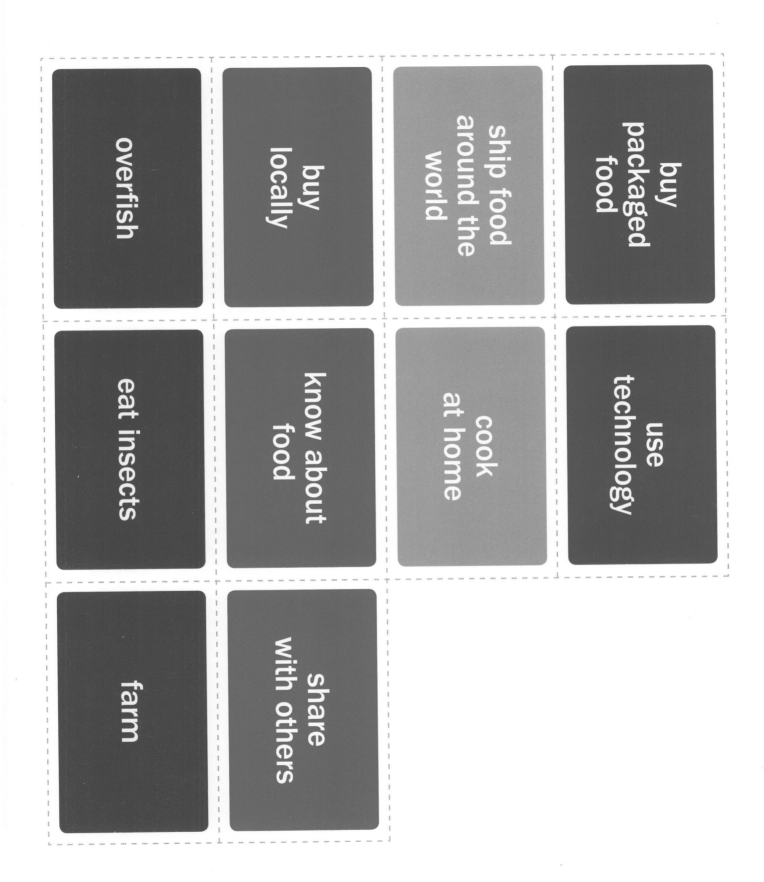

overfish

buy locally

ship food around the world

buy packaged food

eat insects

know about food

cook at home

use technology

farm

share with others

Begin by saying:

Concerts aren't harmful to the environment. People are just there to hear the music.

Correct by saying:

Only 1 in 5 water bottles gets recycled.

Begin by saying:

You don't need reusable bags for shopping. You can just get plastic bags from the shop.

Correct by saying:

Air shows are popular all over the world. Each year, about 600 shows are performed.

Begin by saying:

Air shows can have a negative impact, but they happen so rarely that it isn't a big problem.

Correct by saying:

Many amusement parks use high-efficiency LED lights.

Begin by saying:

Buying bottled water isn't bad for the environment. You just need to recycle the bottles.

Correct by saying:

A single car race uses almost 20,000 litres (5,300 gal.) of fuel.

Begin by saying:

Car racing isn't that bad for the environment. The races are over so fast, they can't possibly use too much fuel.

Correct by saying:

Around 1 trillion plastic bags are consumed each year. Plastic bags can take nearly 1,000 years to break down.

Begin by saying:

Amusement parks use too much energy to light up their rides.

Correct by saying:

People litter at concerts. For example, over 1,600 tonnes of rubbish were left after a single concert in the United Kingdom.

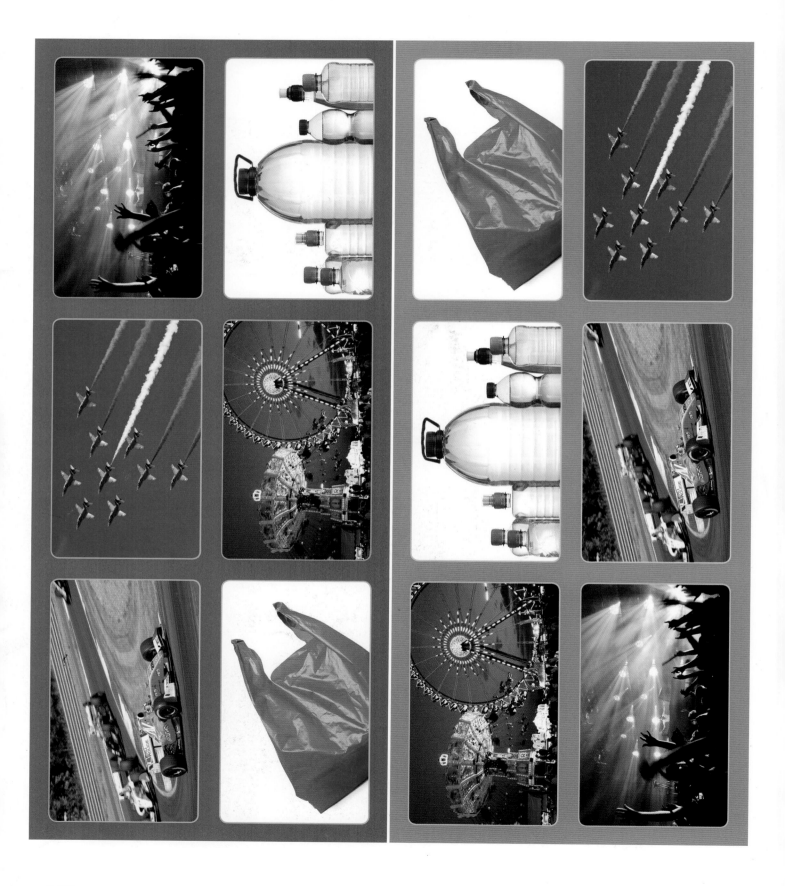

START

Find a venue that's accessible by bus. (think about)

Advertise with social media, not paper. (continue)

There's too much litter to clean up. **LOSE A TURN!**

Invite environmental non-profit-making organisations (recommend)

Sell packaged food. (avoid)

Great job! You found ways to refill water containers. **MOVE AHEAD 3 SPACES!**

Use plastic water bottles. (stop)

You suggest selling bottled water. **GO BACK TO START!**

THE EVENT WAS A SUCCESS! CONGRATULATIONS! **END**

Re-use items from other events. (recommend)

Use recycled paper for posters. (choose)

If you could go anywhere in the world, where would you go?

Would you want to travel to an extreme place, such as the ocean floor? Why or why not?

Why do humans explore?

Which explorer that you've learnt about interests you the most? Why?

Identify an explorer of the past. Where did he/she go? What did he/she discover?

What can we learn about ourselves when we go to new places?

Do you have an explorer in your family? Who is it? Where has this person been?

Would you want to live and study in another country for a year? Why or why not?

If you hosted a student from another country, what would you show him/her?

What obstacles must people overcome to explore new places?

What was the most exciting place you've ever explored? Why?

Would you consider yourself an explorer? Why or why not?

Eugenie Clark

Annie Smith Peck

Amelia Earhart

Mary Kingsley

Lee Berger

Barrington Irving

Sylvia Earle

Corey Jaskolski

travel
Africa
Sierra Leone
Gabon
Ogowe River

fly solo
Atlantic Ocean
Canada
Ireland

climb
Huascarán
Andes
Peru

study sharks
South Pacific Ocean
Sea of Cortez
Mexico

film King Tut's tomb
Egypt
Middle East

lead team of aquanauts
Atlantic Ocean
Bahamas

fly solo
Jamaica
Miami
United States

discover fossils
South Africa
Johannesburg
Southern Hemisphere

The palaeontologist who researches *Spinosaurus* is Nizar Ibrahim.

Great white sharks, who are underwater hunters, can smell a drop of blood up to 5 km. (3 mi.) away.

The manta rays that live in the waters of the Indian Ocean have the largest brain of any fish.

Steve Sillett, who is a giant tree specialist, estimates the President is one of the fastest-growing trees in the world.

Blue whales have enormous tongues that weigh as much as an elephant.

The T. rex, which was the fiercest land predator of its time, had huge jaws and teeth.

Rafflesia, which are found in Indonesia, are giant flowers measuring over 1 m. (3.3 ft.) wide.

The megalodon, which lived more than two million years ago, may have been the largest creature in the sea.

really

so

Kenneth Shinozuka created sensors to help his grandfather and other Alzheimer's patients.

Richard Turere's invention protected his family's cattle from lions.

hardly

rather

Kelvin Doe became a DJ by creating his own radio equipment.

Deepika Kurup invented a solar-powered device that cleans water.

very

kind of

Tan Le helps researchers study the brain with her Emotiv Insight headset.

Sanga Moses brings clean energy to people in Uganda.

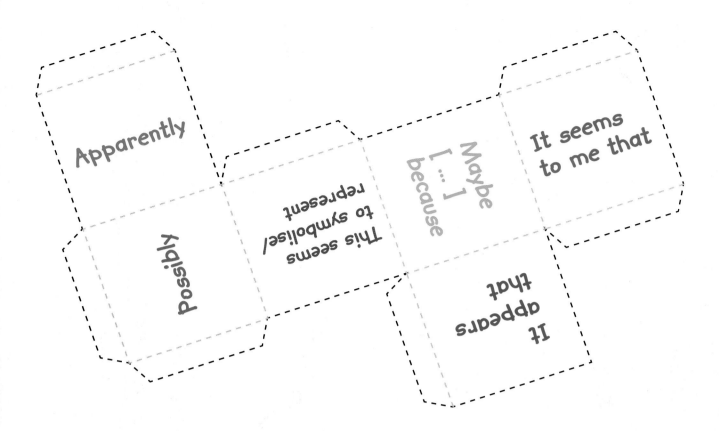

	Painting	Famous Artists	Cave Art	Sculpture	Abstract Art
100	FREE	cut off	stand out	fit in	work out
200	hang up	FREE	work out	put together	look down on
300	track down	give up on	FREE	get across	come up with
400	calm down	throw away	draw in	FREE	give up on
500	put up with	come up against	let (us) in on	rave about	FREE